For Those Left Behind...

Guidance on Death and Grieving

Omar Suleiman

KUBE PUBLISHING

In association with

YAQEEN™
INSTITUTE FOR ISLAMIC RESEARCH

For Those Left Behind…
Guidance on Death and Grieving

First published in England by
Kube Publishing Ltd
Markfield Conference Centre
Ratby Lane
Markfield
Leicestershire
LE67 9SY
United Kingdom

Tel: +44 (0) 1530 249230

Website: www.kubepublishing.com
Email: info@kubepublishing.com

Cataloguing in-Publication Data is available from the British Library.

ISBN 978-1-84774-193-6 Paperback
ISBN 978-1-84774-194-3 Ebook

Cover design and typesetting: Jannah Haque
Printed by: IMAK Ofset, Turkey.

Transliteration

A brief guide to some of the letters and symbols used in the Arabic transliteration in this book.

th	ث	*ḥ*	ح	*dh*	ذ
ṣ	ص	*ḍ*	ض	*ṭ*	ط
ẓ	ظ	ʿ	ع	ʾ	ء
ā	ـَا ـا آ	*ī*	ـِي	*ū*	ـُو

صلى الله عليه وسلم
May the peace and blessings of Allah be upon him.

عز وجل
Glorified and Majestic (is He).

رضي الله عنه
May Allah be pleased with him.

رضي الله عنها
May Allah be pleased with her.

رضي الله عنهما
May Allah be pleased with them both.

عليه السلام
May peace be upon him.

عليها السلام
May peace be upon her.

عليهما السلام
May peace be upon them both.

To Allah belongs that which He has taken, and that which He has given.

And everything is with Allah in accordance with its prescribed time.

So be patient and seek reward [from Allah].

Prophet Muhammad ﷺ

Contents

Introduction vi

1. The *Janāzah* 1
2. The Burial 9
3. The Best *Duʿā's* 17
4. The Best Deeds on Their Behalf 25
5. Where Are They? 37
6. Are They With Each Other? 45
7. Do They Hear Me When I Visit? 55
8. Do They Know What Is Happening to Me? 63
9. What If I Dream About Them? 69
10. Are They Considered *Shuhadā'*? 77
11. Losing a Child 83
12. Condolences 91
13. The Widow 99
14. Women Praying *Janāzah* 107
15. How Do I Move On? 113

Introduction

Fifteen years ago, I lost the most beloved person in the world to me. My mother, May (also spelled Mai) Hashem Suleiman, died suddenly from a stroke leaving behind my father, my brother, and myself. She was a person of piety who longed for her Lord and left the world at peace with it.

But the turmoil in our hearts was, and still is, deep. I was young when my mom died, just appointed as an Imam of a *Masjid*, and between my nikah and wedding. As I sought to understand why, I also sought to exert myself towards what would be of benefit to her and me.

I dove into the works of Ibn al-Qayyim ﵀ and other scholars who spoke of the realm of souls and wondered whether my mom could hear me when I visited her. I wanted so badly to both be connected to her, and to benefit her. I wondered if she knew of my wedding, or now my three children. Many questions flowed through my mind, questions that I would later learn many others shared as well.

Fast forward to 2020, at the peak of the pandemic, many community members passed on. This was especially true of some of our elderly community members who were of course the most vulnerable. As I started to receive question after question, I recognized that pain in the face of many people who were young like me and who, in some cases, lost both parents within days of each other. I realized we needed to put together a resource to help people through this difficult period. Something that would help anyone who experiences the loss of a loved one, and has questions about what happens next and how to move forward.

Our team at Yaqeen quickly pulled together and decided to record the series, "For Those Left Behind", to help people navigate this journey of death and connection after. This book is a result of the research that went into making the video series.

I pray Allah accepts it on behalf of my mom, and on behalf of all of those who have preceded us. May Allah have mercy on our loved ones, allow us to follow them in righteousness, and join us together in His reward.

Āmīn.

Dr. Omar Suleiman
President and Founder
Yaqeen Institute for Islamic Research

1

The Janāzah

You entered this world with the call to prayer (*adhān*) being recited over you, but without any prayer (*ṣalāh*) being performed. When you depart from this world, there will be a prayer read over you, but there will be no call to prayer for it. The contrast between these two epic events has much significance. It is as if to say that the fleeting life which you experience in this world is as short as the duration between the call to prayer and the prayer itself.

While you were still inside the womb of your mother, an angel was appointed to register the duration of your life and the exact date of your death. This paradoxically implies that the moment you enter this world, you are actually already in one sense on your way to exit from it. All of these stark realities constitute a powerful reminder that we should consistently perform our prayers before we are prayed upon. This is because this life is far shorter than we may initially think.

Upon their death, every Muslim is entitled to have the funeral prayer (*ṣalāh al-janāzah*) performed upon them by their fellow believers. Not only is it a religious act of worship, but it is also a way to bid farewell to our loved ones. Furthermore, it constitutes a sobering reminder that we too will one day follow them on the same path. The wise person is the one who always visualises the fateful day when the funeral prayer is offered over their dead body, and allows that thought to shape their life trajectory. The Prophet ﷺ taught us how to perform the funeral prayer in elaborate detail. The prayer is unique in both its form and order, as it consists of four successive *takbīrs*. After the first *takbīr* we are required to recite *Sūrah al-Fātiḥah*. After the second, one should send prayers (*ṣalawāt*) upon the Prophet ﷺ, preferably through a full reading of the *al-Ṣalāh al-Ibrāhīmiyyah*, which we are already accustomed to reciting during our regular prayers. After finishing it, one then reads the third *takbīr*, which should be followed with a *duʿā'* for the deceased. There are a number of confirmed supplications which have all been transmitted from the Prophet ﷺ. Among them is the following:

اللَّهُمَّ اِغْفِرْ لِحَيِّنَا وَمَيِّتِنَا، وَشَاهِدِنَا وَغَائِبِنَا، وَصَغِيرِنَا وَكَبِيرِنَا، وَذَكَرِنَا وَأُنْثَانَا،
اللَّهُمَّ مَنْ أَحْيَيْتَهُ مِنَّا فَأَحْيِهِ عَلَى الإِسْلَامِ، وَمَنْ تَوَفَّيْتَهُ مِنَّا فَتَوَفَّهُ عَلَى الإِيمَانِ

"O Allah, forgive our living ones, deceased ones, present ones, absent ones, our little youngsters, elderly folk, our males, and our females. O Allah, whoever You have decreed to live amongst us, then let them live upon Islam. And whoever You decree to die, then have them die with full faith."

We make this *duʿā’* for the deceased—which was taught to us by the Prophet ﷺ—in a sincere and heartfelt manner during this short and special prayer.

After the fourth *takbīr*, you should make *duʿā’* for yourself and all members of the Ummah. If you wish, you may also further supplicate for the deceased. Some of the scholars have recommended the following supplication at this point:

اللَّهُمَّ لَا تَحْرِمْنَا أَجْرَهُ وَلَا تُضِلَّنَا بَعْدَهُ

"O Allah, do not deprive us of his reward, and do not allow us to go astray after him."

Then the prayer concludes, either with one or two *taslīms*. But before we discuss this latter issue in further detail, I would like to briefly pause and discuss the question of why we recite these supplications in this specific manner during the funeral prayer. The scholars have provided a number of explanations for this unique format. Among them is the fact that the funeral prayer is a shortened form of the regular prayer. Nevertheless, it contains the core elements of the beginning and end of the regular prayer. It contains *Sūrah al-Fātiḥah*, which we recite in the beginning of the five daily prayers, and it ends with prayers on the Prophet ﷺ, which are said at the end. Another form of reasoning is that this special form of prayer encompasses all the key ingredients of a successful *duʿā’*: it contains praise (*ḥamd)* of Allah ﷻ and prayers (*ṣalawāt*) upon the Prophet ﷺ. Only after these two crucial components are met do we make *duʿā’* for our beloved deceased and the Ummah as a whole. By having these prerequisites in place we increase the chances that our supplication will be accepted, as we first praise Allah ﷻ and His Messenger ﷺ. Due to the prayer's brevity, some of the scholars have mentioned that it is to be concluded with a single *taslīm*, because it is not considered to be a complete prayer. This is in fact the position of some schools of thought. However, if you are performing the prayer behind an Imam, then you should follow him however he concludes it, regardless of whether it is finished with one or two *taslīms*.

Most interestingly, the funeral prayer is one of the key rights that a Muslim has upon their fellow Muslim counterparts. This prayer, unbeknownst to many, is of utmost importance since it is a communal obligation. In an important *ḥadīth*, the Prophet ﷺ said that the rights of a Muslim upon another Muslim are five. The first of these rights is responding to a fellow Muslim's greeting (*salām*). Interestingly, in another *ḥadīth*, the Prophet ﷺ mentioned that one of the signs of the Day of Judgement is that the people will only issue greetings to the individuals they know. At that point, it will no longer be considered as a greeting among Muslims, but a salutation that people will only use among the people they recognise, that is, their inner circles. The greeting will no longer be used in an inclusive way, but actually in an exclusivist manner, where people will be neglected from it if they do not meet the additional arbitrary criteria set by different groups. The second right that the Prophet ﷺ mentioned in the *ḥadīth* is visiting the sick. While it is true that during the pandemic it is difficult to observe this Sunnah, one should note that even in regular circumstances this right was neglected by many of us. It is an amazing and beautiful practice to visit sick people simply by virtue of them being Muslim. You are not visiting them because you are forced to or because they are from your close family members; instead, you are comforting them for the sake of Allah ﷻ and also make sincere *duʿā'* for them. The third right that the Prophet ﷺ mentioned was attending and following the funeral procession of a Muslim. To fulfil this right, you must pray the funeral prayer over them and then attend their funeral procession as well. The fourth right which the Prophet ﷺ mentioned was that one should respond positively to their invitations. One will not fulfil this right if they simply respond to the invitations from people of a high class or the members of society that they personally know. The fifth right which the Prophet ﷺ mentioned is that one should pray for their fellow Muslim after they sneeze. When someone sneezes and says *alḥamdulillāh*, you should say to them *yarḥamuk Allāh,* which means, "May Allah have mercy upon you".

These rights are equal and inalienable, which means that they apply to all Muslims. It is incorrect to only uphold these obligations for people of social significance or high ranking. It is true that in technical terms, the funeral prayer is only *farḍ kifāyah*, which renders it to be a communal obligation. It is not actually *farḍ ʿayn,* where the performance of an act is considered an obligation for every single individual. However, one cannot fail to notice the sharp discrepancies in how this prayer is carried out in numbers for different people. Usually, famous figures or individuals with bigger families enjoy larger congregations to carry out their funeral prayer after they pass away. At this point, it is crucial to recall the famous story of the Abyssinian woman who used to clean the *masjid* of the Prophet ﷺ. Conventionally, this story is invoked to indicate the virtue of cleaning the *masjid*.

However, this story can and should be analysed from another angle. For it did not take long for the Prophet ﷺ to notice that the woman was missing; almost immediately after her death he missed her presence. He subsequently asked his Companions ﷺ where she was. The Companions ﷺ responded that she had passed away a night earlier. The Prophet ﷺ became distressed, and inquired why he was not informed of this matter so that he could perform the funeral prayer over her. The Companions ﷺ said that they did not want to bother him, as the timing was inconvenient, so they undertook all her burial rites. At this point, the Prophet ﷺ could have simply indicated his displeasure by stating *lā ḥawla wa lā quwwata illā billāh*, and then leave the matter as it was. However, instead he promptly instructed them: "Guide me to her grave." They all went to her gravesite, and he performed the funeral prayer over her again. He then stated: "These graves are chambers of darkness, and they are lit up by my prayer upon them."

A beautiful lesson which one can derive from this event is that no deceased person should be deemed as being too insignificant for having the funeral prayer performed over them. Unfortunately, in difficult times like these where there are many deaths and funerals, we notice that there are glaring discrepancies in attendance numbers. In addition to the intrinsic right of every Muslim brother or sister having the funeral prayer performed over them, there are also individual incentives which should motivate us to attend every funeral. This is the beauty of our religion, for it further incentivises us to perform acts which we should be already doing in the first place. The Prophet ﷺ said: "The one who prays the funeral prayer will have the reward equivalent to the size of Uḥud. And the one who follows it as well will earn the reward equalling the size of two Uḥuds." Anyone who has had the opportunity to see Uḥud knows how huge of a mountain it is. So if you think the deceased person in question is relatively insignificant, do not allow that fact to prevent you from capitalising on the immense rewards possible. There is yet another significant facet which should be mentioned at this point. After his son passed away, Ibn ʿAbbās ؓ sent Kurayb to investigate and determine how many people attended the funeral. Kurayb reported that the congregation number was considerably big. Ibn ʿAbbās ؓ became pleased and then said: "I heard the Messenger of Allah ﷺ say: 'If a Muslim dies and forty people who worship Allah alone perform the prayer over him, Allah will accept their intercession for him.'" So let us exert our efforts to have large and sincere funeral congregations. No one is insignificant, the incentives are plentiful, and we have the opportunity of becoming intercessors for our brethren in the Hereafter.

While you were still inside the womb of your mother, an angel was appointed to register the duration of your life and the exact date of your death. It's a powerful reminder to consistently perform our prayers before we are prayed upon. This life is far shorter than we may initially think.

2

The Burial

When the Prophet ﷺ passed away, 'Ā'ishah ؓ screamed and cried loudly. When Fāṭimah ؓ heard the weeping of 'Ā'ishah, she realised that the Prophet ﷺ had left this world. At that moment she recited the following beautiful poetic words:

يَا أَبَتَاهُ مِنْ رَبِّهِ مَا أَدْنَاهُ، يَا أَبَتَاهُ إِلَى جِبْرِيلَ أَنْعَاهُ، يَا أَبَتَاهُ جَنَّةُ الفِرْدَوْسِ مَأْوَاهُ

"O my dear father! How close he is now to his Lord.
O my dear father! To Jibrīl we announce his passing.
O my dear father! The Highest Eternal Garden
(Jannah al-Firdaws) is now his abode."

Knowing that a person will die is one thing, but to actually see their soul leave the body is a completely different experience. To wash their dead body is an even more intense, emotional experience. Anyone who has washed the dead will attest to the fact that performing this purification process for someone that they had known has a completely different feeling compared to doing it for an unknown person. Upon washing the body of a friend or loved one, you truly realise the deception and worthlessness of this life, as a dead body lays before you. Before this person's death, you had many priceless memories with them and shared deep emotional moments. You recall all the interactions and conversations you had with that person throughout the years; but now you see this lifeless corpse before you. Because of the impact found in this contrast, you may really begin to cherish the last moments you have with them, as you stand and watch their deceased body. You might gently stroke them or even kiss them on the forehead. In fact, it is narrated that after the Prophet ﷺ passed away, Abū Bakr ؓ kissed his forehead for the last time. In addition, when ʿUthmān ibn Maẓʿūn ؓ passed away, the Prophet ﷺ did the same thing to him; he kissed his forehead and looked at him with deep contemplation.

One of the hardest acts to perform in this world is putting dirt on the face and the other parts of the body of a deceased person. In fact, the whole funeral process involves many difficult steps and stages. First, you see the soul exit the body. Thereafter, you wash the body, comb the hair, and then enshroud and perfume it in preparation for the burial. You give your loved one your last kiss on their head and cherish the final moments with them. Then, as a means of honouring them and allowing their body to rest, you must put dirt on their face. This is undoubtedly a difficult thing to do, but it is a necessary rite in our religion. In fact, we have a moving account where Fāṭimah asked Anas ibn Mālik ؓ a difficult question after the Prophet ﷺ was buried: how did they feel putting the Prophet ﷺ beneath the Earth and burying him? Just imagine you lived more than 1400 years ago, where you were among the Companions ﷺ who buried the Prophet ﷺ and had to put dirt on his face. Furthermore, imagine how difficult it must have been for Anas ﷺ to participate in the burial process. Anas ﷺ had a very close and lengthy relationship with the Prophet both as a child and adolescent; the two had very warm and enjoyable experiences. Fāṭimah framed her question to Anas ﷺ in the following manner:

يَا أَنَسُ أَطَابَتْ أَنْفُسُكُمْ أَنْ تَحْثُوا عَلَى رَسُولِ اللهِ ﷺ التُّرَابَ

"O Anas! How could your souls be content with throwing dirt on the Prophet ﷺ?"

She wanted to know how their hearts and minds felt while burying the Prophet ﷺ, and how they allowed themselves to do such a thing. Anas ﷺ was at first speechless, but he explained that they had to completely ignore the discomfort and pain in their hearts while they buried the Prophet ﷺ under the ground. They felt extreme pain while doing this. It was by no means an easy process, but it was an absolute necessity.

The Prophet's death was the most difficult and heartbreaking scenario, as the Companions ﷺ had the most intimate religious experiences with him and loved him more than anyone else in this world. But it should be noted that in general terms, a person will experience similar emotions of grief and pain whenever they have to bury a loved one.

The Prophetic Sunnah recommends that one hastily bury the body of the deceased after performing the funeral prayer over them.

As a whole, the entire funeral process is swift and uninterrupted. The body is not left out for days in a funeral home or preserved for additional ceremonies after the prayer. Instead, the body is to be taken to the funeral site as fast as possible. In fact, some of the Companions ﷽ mention that for the funeral of Saʿd ibn Muʿādh ﷽, the Prophet ﷺ was proceeding extremely quickly to the funeral site. He walked so quickly that the slippers of the Companions ﷽ would fall off as they tried to keep up with the Prophet's pace.

The righteous soul awaits its final resting place, saying to the people around it:

قَدِّمُونِي قَدِّمُونِي

"Hurry up and take me! Hurry up and take me!"

The wicked soul, on the other hand, is confused and at disarray. It says instead:

يَا وَيْلَهَا إِلَى أَيْنَ تَذْهَبُونَ بِهَا

"O damn! Where are you taking it to?"

After assuming—with Allah's permission—that the deceased person in question was a righteous and noble person, the optimal course of action is to take it to its burial place quickly. When placing the body in its grave, the Sunnah is to state the following:

بِسْمِ اللَّهِ وَعَلَى سُنَّةِ رَسُولِ اللَّهِ

"In the name of Allah, and in the way of the Messenger of Allah."

Likewise, if one wishes, they may also add the following *duʿāʾ*:

اللَّهُمَّ اغْفِرْ لَهُ اللَّهُمَّ ثَبِّتْهُ

"O Allah, forgive them! O Allah, keep them firm!"

These are the supplications that one should recite when one places the dead body in the grave. The Prophetic Sunnah is to first delicately place the feet of the deceased in the grave. Furthermore, the right side of the body should face towards the direction of prayer (*qiblah*). In order to achieve this objective, some additional dirt from the grave spot might have to be taken out. Furthermore, the casket might need to be moved or adjusted to allow it to properly face this direction. Upon burying the deceased, the Prophet ﷺ advised the attendees to observe the following at that moment:

اسْتَغْفِرُوا لأَخِيكُمْ وَسَلُوا لَهُ التَّثْبِيتَ فَإِنَّهُ الآنَ يُسْأَلُ

"Seek forgiveness for your brother, and ask for their steadfastness, for they are now being questioned."

This matter is undoubtedly critical, as the deceased is facing the three most important questions of their lives. It is inappropriate to confidently presume that they are thriving during this state and that everything will be alright. When the deceased is first put into the grave, that is when they feel the tightness and constriction of the grave's sides. That is when they notice the darkness and the cold temperature around them. At that point, they are in the greatest need of support through your *duʿāʾ*; that way, they can be firm and steadfast when the angels question them about their faith and beliefs. They need that spiritual assistance more than anything else. This is why it is common to see the attendees gather and perform a group *duʿā'* for the deceased after they have been buried. Supplicating for the deceased as a group is permissible, even though the Sunnah of the Prophet ﷺ is to have each person offer their own individual *duʿā'*. Making *duʿā'* collectively is permissible, though it should not necessarily take the place of individual supplications. The latter can be stronger and more sincere, especially if a person is making *duʿā'* for their loved ones.

Eulogies or enumerating the praiseworthy qualities of the deceased person will not help them during this critical moment. The concept of eulogising or excessive commendation of the deceased actually has no place in Muslim funerals. In fact, exaggerating in one's praise of the deceased can be counterproductive, and actually prove harmful for the person who has departed from the world. The Prophet ﷺ has mentioned that when people embellish the qualities of a dead person the angels poke that person and ask them:

أَهَكَذَا كُنْتَ

"Are you what they say you were?"

However, one is permitted to mention a deceased person's praiseworthy qualities without any exaggeration. There is no harm in this, for the Prophet ﷺ said the following to his Companions ﷺ specifically and the members of his Ummah in general:

أَنْتُمْ شُهَدَاءُ اللهِ فِي الأَرْضِ

"You are the witnesses of Allah in the Earth."

Thus, to mention the good qualities of the deceased without any exaggeration or the use of embellished formalities is fine. Mentioning a person's noteworthy characteristics in a moderate manner can be beneficial, as the living may derive lessons from them, and at the same time be witnesses of their good actions.

Likewise, the burial procession is not a time where wailing or screaming for the deceased is permissible. These forms of actions must be avoided as much as possible, as they are impermissible. Crying in a quiet and controlled manner, however, is not just a natural and understandable reaction, but it is also a Sunnah of the Prophet ﷺ. As for loudly crying, wailing, or shouting phrases denoting anger and displeasure with Allah's decree, they are to be avoided, as they will actually hurt the dead.

There are additional Sunnahs of the Prophet ﷺ which we should be mindful of as well. One of the established practices of the Prophet ﷺ is to take three handfuls of dirt and scatter it on the dead; every person should partake in this matter and have an opportunity in doing so. Just like how everyone performed four *takbīrs* of prayer over this person, now everyone should have the chance to put three handfuls of dirt. This practice serves as a subtle reminder to the attendees that one day the same ceremony will happen to them as well.

There is now a question of how long the attendees should stay by the gravesite after the burial has been completed. Unfortunately, we usually notice a serious discrepancy in this matter; if the deceased is a person of fame and social standing, then the attendees are plentiful and remain for a pronged period of time.

Otherwise, if the person is relatively unknown, the congregation disperses shortly after the conclusion of the burial. However, there are some reports from the Companions ﷺ which indicate a different standard. For instance, while on his deathbed, ʿAmr ibn al-ʿĀṣ ﷺ requested his family members to stay by his grave after burying him for the duration it takes to sacrifice an animal and distribute its meat. This is a moderate amount of time which does not expire too quickly. This allows family members and friends of the deceased to make additional *duʿā's* for them. ʿAmr then explained the rationale of his specific request; he wanted to feel the presence of his family members (*ḥattā asta'nis bikum*), maintain his confidence and composure, and accordingly respond to the questions posed by the Lord's messengers. By having his family members nearby, he would be able to alleviate his worries and distress under the ground, remain steadfast, and correctly answer the three chief questions posed by the angels.

3

The Best Duʿā's

Abū Hurayrah ﷺ has a moving report which every Muslim should deeply reflect upon. He narrates that after their death, a person will experience an elevation in rank in the sight of Allah ﷻ. Upon being elevated, this person will ask Allah ﷻ:

أَيْ رَبِّ، أَيُّ شَيْءٍ هَذَا

"O my Lord, what is this?"

This man will be surprised, and wonder what the source of this elevation is. Allah ﷻ will then explain this rise in rank with the following answer:

وَلَدُكَ اِسْتَغْفَرَ لَكَ

"Your son sought forgiveness for you."

Reflect for just a moment how beautiful and intricate this connection is. A person's soul will ascend and rise in rank in Paradise as a result of the supplications made on their behalf by their loved ones. Even more interestingly, they will eventually be informed that they received this ascendance as a result of your *duʿāʾ*. There is a very subtle yet thought-provoking benefit in this narration which one should not overlook. We observe that this person's son did not ask Allah ﷻ to raise their parent in rank, but merely asked Him to forgive them. As a general rule, seeking forgiveness (*istighfār*) for the deceased should be our fundamental priority whenever we make *duʿāʾ*. Our supplications should always begin with the following formula:

اللَّهُمَّ اِغْفِرْ لَهُمْ

"O Allah, forgive them."

In fact, we notice that whenever the Prophet ﷺ made *duʿāʾ* for the deceased, he would always ask Allah ﷻ to forgive them first. At this juncture, a person might object and say, "Actually, the deceased person was like an angel and was pure and sincere. They did not do anything wrong in their life. They were without any doubt a flawless individual. Ultimately, they are not in need of our supplications."

This reply is fallacious for a number of reasons. While it is true that we are required to assume well in the case of every Muslim, the stark reality is that we are unaware of the hidden shortcomings and sins that they might have. We can be optimistic and hope that they will be received well by Allah ﷻ, but we ultimately do not know what their standing will be with their Creator.

How do we balance this uncertainty and fear with the good expectation (*ḥusn al-ẓann*) of Allah's treatment of His servants, which we are required to uphold? One may find an answer to this question in the Book of Funerals (*kitāb al-janā'iz*) found in the books of *ḥadīth*, such as al-Bukhārī. In his *Ṣaḥīḥ* collection, al-Bukhārī begins this section with the *ḥadīth* of Abū Dharr. In this narration, the Prophet ﷺ is reported to have said, "Whoever says *lā ilāha illā Allāh* will enter Paradise." In response to this statement, Aū Dharr asked: "Even if he committed adultery and stole?" The Prophet ﷺ said: "Even if he committed adultery and stole." This reply does not in any way lower the magnitude of the sins of adultery and stealing, but they are indicative of the good expectation we are supposed to have of Allah. Even though these sinners may face some forms of punishment in the Afterlife, they will eventually enter Paradise. This is the reason why Imam al-Bukhārī began his section with this particular *ḥadīth*.

The critical point here is that we can never be certain of what shortcomings a person had during their life. In addition, it should be pointed out here that when discussing the connection between seeking forgiveness and elevation in rank, the former is done in many circumstances where a mistake or sin is not known or recognised, even for the case of oneself. For instance, after we conclude our prayers, the first thing we do afterwards is say, "*Astaghfir Allāh, Astaghfir Allāh, Astaghfir Allāh.*" This implies that when seeking Allah's forgiveness, either expiation of a sin or elevation in one's state are sought. The net result is either the blotting away of a sin or an increase in one's good state.

At this juncture, it is necessary for one to realise an important but overlooked fact. As a general rule, our *duʿā's* are most sincere whenever we find ourselves in the most desperate periods of our lives. Now, just briefly reflect on the sheer desperation and vulnerability the deceased person experiences after being buried. After being placed in their grave, the deceased will now be interrogated by the angels and will have to pass the ordeal of the questioning stage. This will undoubtedly be a pivotal moment for them, since the outcome of this interrogation will have huge repercussions for this person's fate. While in the grave, this person cannot make *duʿā'* for themselves or seek Allah's forgiveness. During this crucial time, they can only rely on your sincere *duʿā's* in order to remain strong and steadfast. This fact is of immense significance, and indicates the weighty role and responsibility that attendees of the funeral bear. Making effective and sincere *duʿā'* for the forgiveness of this person should be the priority during this moment. It is incorrect to ignore the urgency of this situation and enumerate the good qualities of the deceased, or simply assume that everything in the Hereafter will be fine for this lost loved one.

Several of these *duʿā's* have been transmitted in the Prophetic Sunnah. One of the most famous and well-known reports is related by ʿAwf ibn Mālik ﵁. He said that he heard the Prophet ﷺ recite the following invocation upon the death of one of his Companions ﵃:

اللَّهُمَّ اِغْفِرْ لَهُ وَارْحَمْهُ ، وَعَافِهِ وَاعْفُ عَنْهُ ، وَأَكْرِمْ نُزُلَهُ ، وَوَسِّعْ مُدْخَلَهُ ، وَاغْسِلْهُ بِالمَاءِ
وَالثَّلْجِ وَالبَرَدِ ، وَنَقِّهِ مِنَ الخَطَايَا كَمَا نَقَّيْتَ الثَّوْبَ الأَبْيَضَ مِنَ الدَّنَسِ

"O Allah, forgive him and have mercy on him, grant him safety and pardon him, and make his reception and settlement place honourable. Expand the entrance of his grave, cleanse him with water, snow, and hail, and purify him of sin as a white robe is purified of dirt."

This is a *duʿāʾ* that a person will most likely hear after the deceased has been buried in their final resting place. It is one of the famous two narrations that have been transmitted from the Prophet ﷺ in this regard. In fact, a person can recite this supplication after the third *takbīr* of the funeral prayer as well. In addition, one is also permitted to recite this invocation in the graveyard, and even immediately after a person has departed from this world.

In other *duʿā's* of the Prophet ﷺ, one will find frequent requests and pleas for mercy, a constant theme which is found in many contemporary *duʿā's* as well. In his supplications, the Prophet ﷺ would often mention the mercy of Allah ﷻ and His lofty attributes before proceeding to state the requests and demands that he had. In fact, one of my favourite and most powerful *duʿā's* on the occasion of death contains these various themes, where the Prophet ﷺ is reported to have said:

اللَّهُمَّ عَبْدُكَ وَابْنُ أَمَتِكَ احْتَاجَ إِلَى رَحْمَتِكَ، وَأَنْتَ غَنِيٌّ عَنْ عَذَابِهِ

"O Allah, this servant and son of a servant is now in need of Your mercy. And You are not in need of punishing that person."

Now, carefully observe the next part of this powerful *duʿā'*:

إِنْ كَانَ مُحْسِناً فَزِدْ فِي حَسَنَاتِهِ، وَإِنْ كَانَ مُسِيئاً فَتَجَاوَزْ عَنْهُ

"If he was righteous and pious, then increase him in rewards and good. And if he was a transgressor, then overlook his faults and pardon him."

This *duʿā'* is extremely short, yet it is rich, all-encompassing, and comprehensive.

The last supplication which I would like to mention in this context has already been cited in the *Angels Series*, but I believe that it deserves to be added here as well. This *duʿā'* was recited after the noble Companion Abū Salamah ﵁ departed from this world. Upon his death, the Prophet ﷺ closed his eyes and said: "Do not make *duʿā'* except for something that will be beneficial, as the angels will say *Āmīn* to what you will say." The Prophet ﷺ urged them to be careful with their words, as Abū Salamah ﵁ had just passed away. Then the Prophet proceeded to supplicate by saying:

اللَّهُمَّ اغْفِرْ لأَبِي سَلَمَةَ وَارْفَعْ دَرَجَتَهُ فِي المَهْدِيِّينَ

"O Allah, forgive Abū Salamah, and raise his rank among those who are rightly guided."

As it can be observed, the Prophet ﷺ began his supplication by being concerned with Abū Salamah's state in the Hereafter. This is the most important priority. Then the Prophet continued his supplication by discussing other matters of importance, such as Abū Salamah's status in the separating metaphysical realm (*barzakh*) and the condition of his descendants:

وَافْسَحْ لَهُ فِي قَبْرِهِ، وَنَوِّرْ لَهُ فِيهِ، وَاخْلُفْهُ فِي عَقِبِهِ فِي الْغَابِرِينَ

"Make his grave spacious for him, and give him light in it. Grant him a successor from his descendants who have been left behind."

If someone carefully evaluates this *duʿā'* and its structure, they will come to the conclusion that it is logically sequenced. First and foremost, it is concerned with Abū Salamah's ultimate destination in the other world. Subsequently, the Prophet ﷺ asks for Abū Salamah's salvation in the Hereafter. The separating metaphysical realm is mentioned afterwards, since it is only a temporary station and a representation of one's place in the other world. This is why the Prophet ﷺ asked Allah ﷻ to raise Abū Salamah's rank with the rightly guided before requesting that his grave be expanded and illuminated. Finally, he made mention of his descendants.

When praying for one's loved ones, one should not always stick to a particular sequence or ordering in one's *duʿā'*. It is true that there will always be constants which must be observed, such as making praise (*ḥamd*) of Allah ﷻ, seeking forgiveness, and sending prayers (*ṣalawāt*) upon the Prophet ﷺ, all of which are dimensions found in the funeral prayer as well. However, it is important to supplicate in a sincere and desperate manner, such that every word comes directly from the heart. Feel free to make *duʿā'* in your own language, if that makes you more comfortable and allows you to express yourself more freely. The deceased person is in urgent need of your *duʿā'*s, especially after being immediately buried.

Whenever the Prophet ﷺ made du'ā' for the deceased, he would always ask Allah عَزَّ وَجَلَّ to forgive them first. It is important to supplicate in a sincere and desperate manner, such that every word comes directly from the heart.

4

The Best Deeds on Their Behalf

A man came to the Prophet ﷺ and mentioned that his mother had suddenly passed away. This ultimately meant that she was unable to give a final will or testament. He then mentioned to the Prophet ﷺ:

لَوْ تَكَلَّمَتْ تَصَدَّقَتْ

"Had she been able to speak, then she would have wanted to give charity."

He then asked the Prophet ﷺ if he could give charity on her behalf. The Prophet ﷺ told him to do so. The reason why I began with this narration is because it provides a very important yet oft-ignored lesson. One should observe this man's carefully thought-out starting point. He was asking himself what his mother's last request and wish would have been if she could speak. He knew that she would not desire a grave decorated with marble, topped with an elevated tombstone. She would not want her gravestone to be engraved with some ornamental writing or a passage from the Qur'ān. Neither would she request his son to burn some incense on top of her grave.

Instead of having you engage in such frivolous and pointless endeavours, what would your deceased loved one actually seek and desire? They would ask you to perform something beneficial on their behalf, such as the distribution of charity and other good deeds. This is because after their death they are in dire need of additional good deeds. In fact, if they could address you directly, they would likely become angry and admonish you to spend money on these worthless acts. After all, many of these pursuits and schemes have no religious benefit whatsoever. Unfortunately, during many funeral processions, one finds exorbitant amounts of wealth being spent on tombstones, grave design schemes, and related matters. Sometimes the level of spending is so great that it can actually be considered sinful in the sight of Allah ﷻ. Ultimately, whenever we do something for the deceased, we should always ask what they would want us to do if they could address us.

At the same time, we should be considerate of metaphysical events that occur in the other realm as well. The Prophet ﷺ mentioned something beautiful and thought-provoking that occurs when a righteous person is in their grave. He stated that while they are buried, they will be suddenly greeted with a special visitor who is exceptionally beautiful, adorned in delightful clothing, and characterised with an extremely pleasant fragrance. Upon approaching the grave, the visitor will address the deceased with the following words:

أَبْشِرْ بِالَّذِي يَسُرُّكَ

"Glad tidings with that which makes you pleased."

The deceased person will then respond by expressing his amazement at the beauty of this face. In fact, he will go on to say:

وجْهُكَ الوَجْهُ يَجِيءُ بِالخَيْرِ

"Your face is definitely the face of the one who comes with good news."

They know that a bearer of bad news or disposer of punishment would not approach them with such an appearance. Quite to the contrary, they will be certain that this person has something positive to convey. In order to determine who this visitor is, they will ask:

مَنْ أَنْتَ

"Who are you?"

They will be wondering: is this a righteous soul, an angel, or some other entity? However, this individual—and may Allah ﷻ make us this individual—will be completely surprised once the visitor reveals his identity:

أَنَا عَمَلُكَ الصَّالِحُ

"I am your good deeds."

A consistent theme that we observe with reference to the Hereafter is that our deeds will be personified. Likewise, our sins and our limbs will become persons who will deliver testimonies against us on the Day of Judgement. May Allah ﷻ protect us from ever using our tongues and limbs in ways which displease Him and incur His wrath. In a parallel fashion, in the other world a person will meet their fasting (*ṣiyām*) and recitation of the Qur'ān as people on the Day of Judgement. They will comfort him and give him good news. Now, at this point reflect on what you would have liked to give this deceased person if they were still alive in this world. You might wish to purchase for them an extravagant piece of jewellery or another gift of tremendous value. You might desire to spend extravagantly so both of you could spend the best day together. While these aspirations may be commendable, they no longer have any value once the loved one has died. They will not be able to benefit from these acts of generosity or kindness. However, your good deeds done on behalf of them will continue to be a source of benefit and will accompany them in their grave. Furthermore, they will be blessed with glad tidings of the special visitors discussed earlier, simply because you bestowed them some additional good deeds. One cannot imagine how pleased they would be with you once they realise that you continued to be a source of goodness for them after they left the world.

On a practical level, there are several things that a person can do to help benefit their deceased loved one. To make the understanding of these different types of actions easier, I will divide them into five different categories. To illustrate these components, I will begin with a pertinent *ḥadīth* which is in many respects similar to the narration mentioned earlier. A woman came to the Messenger of Allah ﷺ and said: "O Messenger of Allah, my mother passed away and she had some outstanding obligatory fasts that she had to make up." The Prophet ﷺ said in response: "Had your mother died with an outstanding debt, would you not have taken care of it and settled it?" The woman said, "Yes." Then the Prophet ﷺ said: "So go ahead and fast on behalf of your mother."

One can then conceptualise outstanding fasts as a form of debt which is to be paid off on behalf of the deceased. If included under this category, this ultimately expands our notion of debts. Otherwise, it could be appropriate to divide debts and deeds into different categories.

Before enumerating the five different categories, it is important to mention an important axiom that has been expressed by a number of scholars: "Glad tidings to the ones who die and their sins die with them." It is never ideal to leave this world without seizing the available opportunities to apologise to the people one has wronged. By failing to do so, one ultimately becomes dependant on others to have their debts repaid and obtain forgiveness from the people they wronged. Each and every one of us should reflect on the gravity of this matter, and be determined to settle any outstanding debts or grievances before we depart from this world, lest we have to depend on others to resolve them. However, if it so happens that one of your loved ones passes away, it is imperative that you conduct a careful investigation into the following matters.

First and foremost, examine whether they had any outstanding debts. Likewise, determine whether they had wronged or harmed any person during their life who has not forgiven them yet. For the former, ensure that you are able to pay the remaining amount to the lender. For the latter case, try to visit the mistreated individual and seek their forgiveness on the deceased's behalf. Be diligent and ask them to forgive your loved one by explaining to them how death is a shocking reminder of the brevity of our lives. Also note how the deceased is now in a vulnerable position and in need of their forgiveness. Through these words of advice, any existing grudges may be eliminated. It is disturbing that just how there is a sharp increase in the use of interest (*ribā*) during the end times, there is likewise a concerning rise in spiritual diseases in the form of grudges and tensions between people. This matter of concern makes it even more imperative for us to search for any people who feel they have an unfulfilled right which should be addressed by the deceased's family.

Secondly, investigate whether they have any outstanding debts that must be paid to Allah ﷻ, such as outstanding acts of worship. I do not intend to downgrade this category by placing it one number below the debts that are to be repaid to people. Instead, the crucial point being indicated here is that it should be a priority to ensure the deceased meets Allah ﷻ while having nothing left outstanding between themselves and the people. That way, they will stand before Allah ﷻ, where the only rights that remain are those between themselves and their Creator.

The debts that must be paid to Allah ﷻ refer to unfulfilled obligations which must be done for the deceased. This most often occurs with the obligatory ritual of Hajj, where a loved one departs from this world without having the chance to perform it. As a result, a living relative performs Hajj on the deceased's behalf once they have had the chance to perform the obligatory (*farīḍah*) pillar for themselves first. Likewise, the same is done in the case of fasting (*ṣiyām*), which was the example addressed by the Prophet ﷺ when he advised the woman. For this case, any missed obligatory fasts which the deceased was unable to make up during their life are to be done on their behalf. It is important to note that every person should inform their relatives or loved ones if they have any missed fasts that are to be made up. This is so that if they suddenly pass away, their loved ones will know whether any fasts have to be made, and then undertake them on their behalf. However, there is one act of worship which can never be made up, and that is the prayer (*ṣalāh*). This is because unlike other acts of worship, the prayer is an obligation at all times, regardless of one's circumstances. Hajj only becomes an obligation if someone has the financial and physical capability; some of these conditions may not be met during a person's life. In a similar fashion, in the case of fasting, there will be circumstances where a person will have to make up for missed days. However, in stark contrast, there are no circumstances where one is allowed to miss the prayer. As long as a person is conscious, they are required to perform the prayer even if only with their eyes and through similar gestures. Once a person loses their consciousness, then the obligation of performing the prayer drops. If it so happened that the deceased left prayers while being in a state of consciousness, then there is no way for a living relative to fulfil that missed obligation on their behalf. We have now been able to adequately discuss the first two categories: debts to the people, and debts to Allah ﷻ.

We can now discuss the realm of deeds, which will be further divided into three categories to make them easy to remember. The first of these three categories—and the third on our list—pertains to the deeds that are an extension of the good that the deceased taught or inspired us to do throughout their lives.

Whenever we perform a good deed, for instance, the Prophet ﷺ always receives a share of that reward. This is because had it not been for the Messenger of Allah ﷺ, we would not have known how to pray or even connect to our Lord at a basic level. This means that the Prophet ﷺ will be given a share of the blessings and rewards that are provided for every good deed. Likewise, whenever a person acts on a *ḥadīth* which legislates a good deed, all of the narrators who transmitted the report—not just the Companion at the end of the chain—will be rewarded for the good they inspired by relating the teachings of the Prophet ﷺ.

If a parent teaches their child an act of good (*ḥasanah*) or a person imparts beneficial lessons and reminders to their community or circle of friends, the original guide will obtain a reward every time the learner acts on these teachings. This is even the case if the child or student does not actively intend that the transmitter of knowledge be rewarded. Whenever one performs the action taught or passed down to them, they do not need to intend that they wish to benefit their teacher or other source of guidance; the mere commission of the act leads to the transfer of rewards to that person. This is undoubtedly one of the greatest manifestations of the mercy of Allah ﷻ, which is unlike anything we can fathom or imagine. Continue to be a source of good and uphold righteous conduct with your parents and other sources of guidance. Making progress in sincerity and religiosity will allow these elders to realise progress as well in the sight of Allah ﷻ.

The fourth category undoubtedly encompasses the largest number of deeds. These are the good deeds which have been specifically legislated in the Prophetic Sunnah. In other words, these are deeds which the Prophet ﷺ specifically said will benefit a person after their death. Without any doubt, one of these acts is making *duʿāʾ*, which we already discussed previously. As noted, it is important to always begin one's *duʿāʾ* by seeking forgiveness (*istighfār*). Another act which was stressed by the Prophet ﷺ in this regard is charity (*ṣadaqah*). The best form of charity is that which is continuous (*ṣadaqah jāriyah*), that is, where its benefits continue to flow over time. For instance, the Prophet instructed Saʿd ibn ʿUbādah ؓ to construct a well for his deceased mother. Saʿd ibn ʿUbādah ؓ even went on to donate a garden for his mother. Without any doubt, the projects which confer an ongoing benefit are the optimal acts of charity which one should prioritise and capitalise on. However, there is no doubt that any type of charity done on behalf of the deceased will be accepted, with the permission of Allah ﷻ.

It is worth noting that in this context the *duʿāʾ* of a righteous child is weightier and more effective than the *duʿāʾ* of anyone else. So far we have mentioned the importance and effectiveness of these two acts: *duʿāʾ* and charity, especially that which is continuous. In addition, one may perform Hajj or *ʿUmrah* on behalf of a deceased person, even if they have already performed the obligatory rites for themselves. In fact, in one of the groups I was leading I found a person who was performing Hajj on behalf of Imam al-Nawawī ؒ. Upon discovering this startling fact, I said: "*Subḥānallāh*, why Imam al-Nawawī r?" The student said in response: "Because *Riyāḍ al-Ṣāliḥīn* changed my life." This person had already performed Hajj multiple times for themselves, and now wanted to perform it on behalf of none other than

Imam al-Nawawī ﷺ. So if you would like to perform Hajj or *ʿUmrah* for a deceased family member or loved one, this is something that Allah has permitted you to do if you have already performed these rites for yourself. That way, we can maintain a spiritual connection with our loved ones in a manner which is sanctioned in the religion as well.

The dissemination of beneficial knowledge is another category worthy of discussion. In order to be a beneficiary of this category, one must contribute towards an intellectual cause which provides everlasting benefits. This can be achieved by constructing a school or funding a noble *daʿwah* initiative on behalf of the deceased. The Prophet ﷺ also stressed that a person should visit and honour the family and friends of the deceased. This is in fact something which the Prophet did with the loved ones of Khadījah ﷺ after the latter had passed away, by always sending them gifts on her behalf. Likewise, ʿAbdullāh ibn ʿUmar ﷺ would honour the children of his father's friends as a means of honouring his own father. All of these deeds are legislated in the Sunnah of the Prophet ﷺ, and they broadly fall within the category of *duʿā'*, charity, and the dissemination of beneficial knowledge. One can either undertake or fund an initiative which imparts knowledge on behalf of the dead person. However, it would not be acceptable to pay a person to make *duʿā'* on behalf of the deceased.

The fifth category encompasses all the other good deeds which are done on their behalf. These refer to deeds which are not specified in the Prophetic Sunnah, but still are known to have rewards, such as reciting the Qur'ān or offering a voluntary act of worship (*nāfilah*) on their behalf. Whether or not the reward of these virtuous deeds reaches the deceased (*īṣāl al-thawāb*) is an issue of contention. The scholars agree that a person can make a specific *du'ā'* for the deceased after completing the recitation of the Qur'ān (*khatm*). But there is a difference of opinion on whether the rewards of unspecified deeds are transferred to the dead. There are some categories of deeds which were not specifically mentioned or discussed by the Prophet ﷺ. On this matter, through the use of analogical reasoning a large number of scholars mentioned that the rewards of all good deeds can be transferred to the deceased. The only conditions for this transfer to be valid are that the good deeds in question be sanctioned and legislated in the religion, and that it be performed with the right intention.

However, it is important to stick to the Prophet's example as much as possible and perform the actions he explicitly specified. If someone wishes to perform other righteous acts as well, that too will be valid and accepted by Allah. But it is imperative to avoid ritualising the performance of these good deeds in a way not sanctioned in the religion. This is now no longer a difference of opinion, but a blameworthy matter altogether. Unfortunately, it is common to find that in some cultures particular acts and rituals are performed 10 or 40 days after a person has passed away. Even further ceremonies are held on the one year mark of their departure. These types of gatherings and practices have no basis in the religion, and should be avoided.

To summarise, the five categories of deeds which must be considered after a person passes away are:

1. Debts to people.
2. Debts to Allah.
3. Righteous deeds which are an inspiration or extension of a person's good deeds.
4. Righteous deeds specified in the Sunnah.
5. Righteous deeds not specified in the Sunnah.

May Allah ﷻ accept all the righteous deeds and actions we perform on behalf of our loved ones.

Where Are They?

Without any doubt, observing a body which has been badly mutilated has a serious psychological toll on a person. This topic is far more difficult to discuss than the previous ones, especially since the initial issues pertained to the blessings and treatment a righteous believer will receive after their death. But once discussing death, one can never ignore the point about how fragile the human body is. This is especially the case if the body has undergone horrific damage through a car accident, or been badly mistreated through mutilation, for instance.

One cannot imagine the difficulties and pains that the Muslims experienced in the aftermath of the Battle of Uḥud. Without any doubt, Uḥud was a very unique experience for the Muslims, as they never experienced a conflict like that in their history. For instance, the way the chief of the martyrs (*sayyid al-shuhadā'*) Ḥamzah ☙ was killed and mutilated was absolutely gruesome.

In the aftermath of this battle, the Prophet ﷺ comforted the devastated believers by sharing with them the following good news: "When your brothers were killed, Allah ﷻ put their souls in the bodies of green birds." He further mentioned that their souls—which are now situated in the bodies of these birds—freely fly over the rivers of Paradise (*Jannah*), and eat from its blessed fruits. They also nestle themselves inside lamps of gold under the shade of Allah's Throne. One cannot imagine how pleasant and satisfying their experience in the other world must be. Not only do they enjoy the eminent rank of being from among the martyrs of Uḥud (*shuhadā' Uḥud*), but they are also now blessed with this incredible state of existence, where they have the freedom to go wherever they wish in Paradise.

What even further beautifies this spectacle is that they are honoured with the presence of Ḥamzah رضي الله عنه, the chief of the martyrs. While enjoying the sweetness of Allah's reward, as well as resting and marvelling at the incredible existence they found themselves in, they actually asked: "Who is going to tell our brothers that we are alive in Paradise?" They wanted their fellow Muslims to know the pleasant and blessed state they found themselves in. Furthermore, it was important for their brothers to know about their salvation so that they would maintain a steadfast posture in battles and not be discouraged from continuing to strive in the path of Allah ﷻ. Lastly, the people of Madinah were in a sorrowful state in the battle's aftermath, and there were large gatherings where the mourners were wailing over the dead bodies of their loved ones. These martyrs were aware of the sorrow of their community, and wanted to alleviate their pain by conveying to them the blissful state they were in. However, the main question was: how would they be able to inform their community of their current state? Allah ﷻ informed the martyrs that He Himself would undertake this task by saying:

أَنَا أُبَلِّغُهُمْ عَنْكُمْ

"I will tell them on your behalf."

Essentially, Allah ﷻ informed the martyrs that He would let the Companions ﷺ know about their current state. He did this by revealing this verse from *Sūrah Āl 'Imrān*:

وَلَا تَحْسَبَنَّ الَّذِينَ قُتِلُوا فِي سَبِيلِ اللَّهِ أَمْوَاتًا ۚ بَلْ أَحْيَاءٌ عِندَ رَبِّهِمْ يُرْزَقُونَ فَرِحِينَ بِمَا آتَاهُمُ اللَّهُ
مِن فَضْلِهِ وَيَسْتَبْشِرُونَ بِالَّذِينَ لَمْ يَلْحَقُوا بِهِم مِّنْ خَلْفِهِمْ أَلَّا خَوْفٌ عَلَيْهِمْ وَلَا هُمْ يَحْزَنُونَ

"Never think of those martyred in the cause of Allah as dead. In fact, they are alive with their Lord, well provided for—rejoicing in Allah's bounties and being delighted for those yet to join them. There will be no fear for them, nor will they grieve."[1]

Some scholars mention that for this Qur'ānic passage, fear (*khawf*) is a reference to anything which comes prospectively while grieving, i.e. that which is left behind. In a similar verse, Allah ﷻ describes how the angels will comfort the believing people—may Allah ﷻ make us among them—when they proceed to take their souls at the point of death:

أَلَّا تَخَافُوا وَلَا تَحْزَنُوا

"Do not fear, nor grieve."[2]

---

1 *Āl 'Imrān*, 169–70.

2 *Fuṣṣilat*, 30.

If one adopts the explanation alluded to above, the angels mean by this statement: "Do not be afraid of what is to come, and do not grieve over that which you have left behind."

One simply cannot cease reflecting over the wonderful state of the martyrs. It makes great sense to begin this discussion with the martyrs, since they enjoy an incredible state of existence. They have their souls inside the bodies of green birds, which are, without any doubt, different from the birds of this world. They are already in a state of bliss, and find themselves in a delightful dimension which represents a form of Paradise, but not its entire totality. During this state they are nestled under the throne of Allah in these splendid golden lamps. These facts provide us some crucial context to the events that revolved around the death of the eminent Companion Saʿd ibn Muʿādh ﵁. When Saʿd passed away, the Prophet ﷺ said:

اِهْتَزَّ عَرْشُ الرَّحْمَنِ لِمَوْتِ سَعْدِ بْنِ مُعَاذٍ

"The Throne of the Most Merciful shook upon the death of Saʿd ibn Muʿādh."

The scholars explained this *ḥadīth* by noting that this shaking did not occur due to trauma or fear. It is incorrect to deduce from this report that this event occurred because the death of Saʿd ibn Muʿādh ﵁ somehow disturbed the equilibrium of the universe and the state of overall existence. Nor can one say it was like the tree which the Prophet used to give his sermon (*khuṭbah*) close to, which cried when he left it and used a pulpit instead. Instead, this event was an expression of joy that the soul of Saʿd ﵁ was going to return to its Lord. Allah had already prepared for Saʿd's soul a perfectly nestled golden lamp which it would inhabit.

Up to this point the discussion has centred around the souls of the martyrs. However, it is also important to discuss the souls of righteous people and determine where their place will be. At the same time, however, it is important to note that the martyrs occupy a special place in the sight of Allah ﷻ. Regarding the *ḥadīths* which mention the state of the souls in Paradise, some scholars argued that they are specific to the martyrs, while others have stated that they refer to the believers in general. An intermediate camp argued that these reports concern the special believers, among whom the martyrs are the best. A *ḥadīth* which relates to this matter is that of the divine night journey (*al-Isrā' wa al-Miʿrāj*), where the Prophet ﷺ ascended to Paradise and met the souls of the Prophets ﷺ there. But at the same, the Prophet ﷺ said:

مَرَرْتُ عَلَى مُوسَى وَهُوَ قَائِمٌ يُصَلِّي فِي قَبْرِهِ

"I passed by Mūsā while he was praying in his grave."

The question then is how these reports are to be explained and reconciled. To do so, it is imperative to analyse the *ḥadīth* which discusses the initial point where the believer enters their grave. In one of the narrations in this matter, the Prophet ﷺ described this crucial moment with the following statement:

ثُمَّ يُفْسَحُ لَهُ فِي قَبْرِهِ

"Then Allah expands for them their grave."

In one of the authentic versions of this narration, he specifies the dimensions of this expansion by stating it is:

سَبْعُونَ ذِرَاعًا فِي سَبْعِينَ

"...seventy cubits by seventy cubits..."

It is unclear whether this expansion occurs in a tangible and physical manner, or in an indiscernible metaphysical realm only. This is a matter of disagreement among the scholars.

Then, the Prophet ﷺ further described the setting of this righteous person's grave by stating:

ثُمَّ يُنَوَّرُ لَهُ فِيهِ

"Then [the grave] in which they reside is lit up."

One here observes an immediate parallel with the *duʿā'* that the Prophet ﷺ made after the death of Abū Salamah ؓ, which consisted of the following words:

وَافْسَحْ لَهُ فِي قَبْرِهِ، وَنَوِّرْ لَهُ فِيهِ

"Make his grave spacious for him, and give him light in it."

While this latter report only mentions the supplication, the former shows the blessed effects of it. The grave expands seventy cubits by seventy yards, and is even blessed with a light. After these transformations in the grave, the deceased person is told the following:

نَمْ

"Now go to sleep."

This person is blessed and has found their true home. They have just entered a chamber of Paradise, where they will find themselves in a blissful state. Yet, during this state, the angels order him to sleep. In response, the person poses a number of questions, which include:

أَرْجِعُ إِلَى أَهْلِي فَأُخْبِرُهُمْ

"Can I go back to my family and inform them?"

This person desires to go back to his family and inform them that he is in a pleasant state, so they will not worry or be concerned about him. It would make them very pleased to find out that their deceased loved one had their grave expanded after passing the test, by successfully answering the three posed queries. They would be even more delighted to know that his grave became an illuminated garden which exudes the scent of Paradise, thanks to their collective *du'ā's* and prayers. They would have their faith increased by knowing that the promise of Allah ﷻ is true. The person eagerly seeks to momentarily return to his family and convey this information and good news. This is obviously an understandable sentiment, since the deceased saw their family members cry for them during the funeral and then had to face the most difficult test ever. In response to his requests, the angels say:

نَمْ كَنَوْمَةِ الْعَرُوسِ الَّذِي لَا يُوقِظُهُ إِلَّا أَحَبُّ أَهْلِهِ إِلَيْهِ

"Sleep like the newlywed person who is only awaken by their most beloved ones."

In essence, this person's grave has become—with the permission of Allah ﷻ—a manifestation of Paradise for them. In fact, the Prophet ﷺ mentioned that this person will be shown their actual place in Paradise twice a day, once in the morning and later on in the evening. In contrast, a wicked person's grave will be a chamber of fire, where they will face a severe punishment in a continuous manner. May Allah protect us all from this latter fate. *Allāhumma Āmīn*.

A number of tentative conclusions can be derived regarding the nature and location of the souls after death. The Prophet ﷺ has clearly indicated to us that some souls will be placed inside the bodies of green birds. In another narration, he mentioned how he once met Mūsā ﵇ during the divine nightly ascent, while in another scenario he met him praying by his grave. Yet, in another narration, the expanded dimensions of the grave are mentioned. These reports can be reconciled by assuming that a person's soul has a connection with their gravesite specifically and the physical world in general. However, at the same time, a person is no longer restricted to the dimensions of this world, in an analogous way to how the soul is no longer confined to the physical dimensions of the body. While a connection remains with the grave, realities are no longer confined to time and space as they are in the physical world. We ask Allah ﷻ to allow us to be blessed by having our souls placed in the bodies of green birds which are nestled in gold lamps under His throne. We also ask Him to allow our souls to roam freely in Paradise, where they can enjoy the delights of its rivers and fruits.

6

Are They With Each Other?

I still vividly recall the first time I had to leave the city of Madinah. At that point I immediately remembered the story of Bilāl ﵁, and how he could no longer bear remaining in the city of Madinah after the Prophet ﷺ had passed away. Bilāl ﵁ faced immense difficulties whenever he attempted to make the call of prayer (*adhān*), since whenever he looked at a certain place or sight, he remembered a moment that he shared with the Prophet ﷺ. This troubled him so much that he requested Abū Bakr ﵁ to send him out in battle for one of their expeditions. He did not give the call of prayer anymore until ʿUmar ﵁ conquered and entered Jerusalem. After that, Bilāl ﵁ resumed giving the call of prayer there, just like he used to in Madinah.

This episode is of immense significance, since it indicates that what bothered Bilāl was not that he could no longer stay in Madinah. The real issue that he faced was that he could no longer remain anywhere in the world without the Prophet ﷺ. This may be somewhat difficult for individuals living in the contemporary world to understand. After all, we cherish the opportunity to go to Madinah, as we know the Prophet's grave and his relics are located there. However, the affair was completely different for the Companions ﷺ. They were blessed to see and interact with the Prophet ﷺ in person for years, and witnessed him live on the Earth in his own flesh and blood. One cannot imagine how difficult it must have been for them to lose him and then live in Madinah without his presence. For Bilāl ﷺ, this loss must have been exceptionally difficult, as there were numerous years between the Prophet's death and Bilāl's appointed time to depart from the world. In fact, Bilāl ﷺ lived on until the time of the plague of 'Amwās. When he was on his deathbed, his wife was crying intensely, and was continuously yelling the following word:

وَاحُزْنَاه

"What a sorrowful day this is!"

In response, Bilāl ﷺ said:

بَلْ قُولِي وَا فَرَحَاهُ، غَدًا نَلْقَى الأَحِبَّةَ مُحَمَّداً وَحِزْبَهُ

"Instead say, 'What a great day this is!' Tomorrow, I will be able to meet my beloved ones: Muhammad and his Companions."

He could not wait to meet the Prophet ﷺ once again. The issue was not just about being in Madinah in a geographic sense, nor merely perceiving the imagery of the Prophet ﷺ by cherishing memories in the city. Neither would saying the call of prayer fill up this void. Instead, ever since the Prophet ﷺ departed from this world, Bilāl was intensely longing for the moment to be united with him once again.

Likewise, one can detect the same emotions and longing with other Companions ﷺ vis-à-vis the Prophet ﷺ as well. When our mother ʿĀ'ishah ﷺ was on her deathbed, one could only imagine the deep emotional state she found herself in. She immensely loved the Prophet and, as his wife, she had a strong emotional bond with him. When she was close to passing away, Ibn ʿAbbās ﷺ entered in order to pay a visit. In reality, ʿĀ'ishah ﷺ did not want Ibn ʿAbbās ﷺ to come during this critical moment, as she knew that he was endowed with eloquence and would likely shower her with words of praise. During her final moments, ʿĀ'ishah ﷺ wanted to spend her time seeking forgiveness (*istighfār*), as well as increasing her state of consciousness of Allah (*taqwā*). She was worried that Ibn ʿAbbās ﷺ might inadvertently ruin this moment of spiritual contemplation.

Nevertheless, Ibn ʿAbbās ﷺ entered and addressed ʿĀ'ishah ﷺ by saying, "How are you, my mother?" ʿĀ'ishah ﷺ responded with a beautiful answer by saying: "I am fine as long as I am in a state where I am conscious of Allah." With this carefully worded reply she wanted to indicate to Ibn ʿAbbās ﷺ that it was her objective to seek forgiveness during these final moments of her life. She did not want to be praised in any manner.

However, Ibn ʿAbbās ﷺ persisted and began praising ʿĀ'ishah ﷺ indulgently. He began to enumerate her different praiseworthy qualities and virtues (*faḍā'il*), such as her status as the favourite wife of the Prophet ﷺ, or the person whom Allah ﷻ directly exonerated through His own Book. He also mentioned how the Prophet ﷺ would always undertake his missions and journeys with her company alone, and even reminded her of the special intimate moments that she and the Prophet ﷺ shared together. He also mentioned the special ways the Prophet ﷺ addressed her. He continued doing this for a while, and then said to her:

أَبْشِرِي، يَا أُمِّي

"Glad tidings, O my mother."

He explained what he meant by this statement by adding:

مَا بَيْنَكِ وَبَيْنَ أَنْ تَلْقَيْ مُحَمَّدًا ﷺ وَالأَحِبَةَ، إِلَّا أَنْ تَخْرُجَ الرُّوحُ مِنَ الجَسَدِ

"Nothing is left between you being reunited with the Prophet ﷺ except for your soul to leave your body."

In essence, he was alluding to the fact that the only barrier that stood between her and the Prophet ﷺ was death; all that was needed for this meeting to take place was for her soul (*rūḥ*) to leave the body (*jasad*). No one can doubt how much ʿĀ'ishah ﷺ longed to see the Prophet ﷺ again, as he had died in her lap and was buried in her room.

Stories regarding the departure of the soul have huge spiritual and theological implications. In fact, Ibn al-Qayyim ﷺ mentions that the righteous souls are able to visit one another and even discuss between themselves events that occurred in the world. In fact, he adds that their movements and encounters are more free and fluid than they were in this world. Ibn al-Qayyim ﷺ further mentions that in the *barzakh*—a metaphysical realm separating this life and the next—every soul keeps the company of those it loved and emulated. This is an extremely powerful point, and is consistent with *ḥadīth*s which have been narrated on this topic. For example, the Prophet ﷺ provided this interesting description of the state of the souls in the pre-worldly spiritual realm:

الأَرْوَاحُ جُنُودٌ مُجَنَّدَةٌ فَمَا تَعَارَفَ مِنْهَا اِئْتَلَفَ، وَمَا تَنَاكَرَ مِنْهَا اِخْتَلَفَ

"The souls are like conscripted soldiers. Those which had an affinity to one another (in the realm of souls) will have a natural affinity to one another (in this world). And those which have a natural aversion to one another (in the realm of souls) will have a natural aversion (in this world)."

This *ḥadīth* is making a reference to the first iteration of interactions that occurred between the souls in the pre-worldly metaphysical realm. In this spiritual world (*ʿālam al-arwāḥ*), the righteous souls were together in a specific group, while the wicked souls had their own separate assembly. In this world we are subject to many physical constraints or limitations, where we may be unable to correspond or unite with a person who shares our characteristics, likes, priorities, and faith commitments. However, once the souls exit their physical bodies and enter the second round of the metaphysical realm, all such restrictions collapse. The Prophet ﷺ alluded to this point in an important *ḥadīth*:

أَنْتَ مَعَ مَنْ أَحْبَبْتَ

"You are with who you love."

One will be with those one loves, that is, the ones they met and developed relationships with in this world, and those who one did not have the chance to see. In other words, in the spiritual dimension, one will have the opportunity to interact and accompany people one never saw in the physical realm found in this world. This is why the believing souls (*arwāḥ al-mu'minīn*) will gather and interact with one another. It is every Muslim's hope that their loved ones and other righteous figures will be there to greet and receive them. Of course, the greatest hope in this dimension is that one will have the opportunity to see and be welcomed by the Prophet ﷺ and his Companions ﵃, who are the ones every Muslim adores and reads about on a consistent basis. Furthermore, one also prays that the Prophet's noble household ﵃ will also be there to greet the community of the believers.

This aforementioned viewpoint is corroborated by several authentic *ḥadīth*s. For instance, there is a *ḥadīth* in which the Prophet ﷺ mentions that the soul will ascend to the seventh level (*'illiyyīn*) in Paradise, which is the uppermost point. Here it will be registered before Allah ﷻ, and will be given the status of a righteous soul. The angels will carry this soul and pass it through the different gates of Paradise. While the righteous soul—may Allah ﷻ make us from the righteous—is ascending, the angels make the following statement in amazement:

مَا أَطْيَبَ هَذِهِ الرِّيحُ الَّتِي جَاءَتْكُمْ مِنَ الأَرْضِ

"What a beautiful scent that has come from the Earth!"

It is an established fact that righteous souls exude a pleasant smell. For instance, the Prophet ﷺ smelled the scent of the hairdresser of the daughter of Firʿawn—who was a righteous woman—during the divine night journey (*al-Isrā' wa al-Miʿrāj*).

After the righteous soul has been registered, the person is able to settle into their new home: the grave. Of course, this transition occurs only after a person has been dressed, has had their surroundings expanded, been provided a shining light, and shown their prospective spot in Paradise. After all these steps are completed, the righteous visitors are then able to come. Regarding this matter, the Prophet ﷺ said:

فَيَأْتُونَ بِهِ أَرْوَاحَ الْمُؤْمِنِينَ، فَلَهُمْ أَشَدُّ فَرَحًا بِهِ مِنْ أَحَدِكُمْ بِغَائِبِهِ يَقْدُمُ عَلَيْهِ

"The souls of the believers gather to receive that person, and they are more delighted to see you than one of you when you receive your long lost loved one."

Such is the affair of the souls of the believers. The souls of those you miss and those whom you never met will come to greet you one by one. At that moment, you will be able to see the righteous people who were your companions and fellow worshippers from the *masjid*. They will all be eagerly waiting for you. Then after meeting you and engaging in discussions, they will begin to ask:

مَاذَا فَعَلَ فُلَانٌ، مَاذَا فَعَلَ فلانٌ

"What happened to so-and-so? And what happened to so-and-so?"

They will continue to pose questions of this nature. Everyone will attempt to retrieve news regarding the physical world, as they will at this point be disconnected from it. One can imagine how within a family unit or group of friends some members can pass away, while the rest of the group remains alive in the existing world. For this reason, questions will be posed concerning the affairs of the existing members. In fact, as Abū Hurayrah notes, even more direct and specific queries will be posed, such as whether an existing family member was able to marry or not. Likewise, they will request information about a family's current state of affairs. These details found in the narration yield an important benefit: the souls in the other realm still have the memories of this world preserved. The different souls will pepper the recently deceased member with a myriad of questions, with every one of them trying to get their attention. This will continue until some of the souls will object and say:

دَعُوهُ ؛ فَإِنَّهُ كَانَ فِي غَمِّ الدُّنْيَا

"Leave them alone, since they were only recently facing the hardships of this world."

These compassionate souls will ask the others to allow the newly deceased soul to rest, as they had to face a tiring experience and difficult transition in order to come to this world. They should ultimately be given some resting time before being bombarded with queries.

When the questions and discussions proceed, shocking and terrifying discoveries are made. The souls begin to ask about certain individuals, and the recently deceased will reply in confusion: "Did that person not already die and come to you?" The recently deceased member will note that the mentioned individual already died before them, and must have arrived earlier. As the discussion progresses, they eventually begin to realise that this person's soul never joined their ranks. Ultimately, the group of souls will say in response:

مَا جِيءَ بِرُوحِ ذَاكَ إِلَيْنَا

"That person's soul was not brought to us."

This leads to a shocking and saddening discovery. If the soul of this person is not with the righteous, then the only logical conclusion can be the following:

قَدْ ذُهِبَ بِهِ إِلَى أُمِّهِ الهَاوِيَةِ

"That person must be among the tormented souls."

This inference is drawn since as a part of their punishment, the tormented souls are deprived from being able to unite with their loved ones. Such a realisation must be saddening and chilling for all the righteous souls, as one of their loved ones will be forever separated from them.

What is frightening is that any one of us can be that separated and punished soul, as our fate in the next life is unknown to us. None of us want to be deprived of enjoying the opportunity of being united with the other righteous souls, but the possibility remains that we can be relegated to the other group. There could be a soul from three years ago and another soul which died last year asking about the status of a person who died in a time frame between them. If that person is missing, they will say, "*Subḥānallāh*, this person is missing! *Innā lillāhi wa innā ilayhi rājiʿūn!*"

You could be that missing person. This is not said to instil despair, but it is a serious reminder that we must strive to do good in order to join those who preceded us in righteousness. If we want to be part of those other-worldly blessed gatherings with the Prophet ﷺ and other members of the righteous folk, we must create and foster the most morally upright versions of ourselves as soon as possible. Otherwise, we will be merely people who dream to join their ranks, but fail to exert the necessary efforts.

7

Do They Hear Me When I Visit?

We cannot supersede the Prophet ﷺ in anything which pertains to religious goodness (*iḥsān*). The first part of this series discussed the various rights that one Muslim has upon another, such as visiting them or performing the funeral prayer over them. These rights and obligations were always observed by the Prophet with the utmost loyalty and courtesy, such that he was the ideal standard to be emulated by the rest of his Ummah. A great example of the Prophet's dedication to the members of his Ummah can be found in the famous story of the Abyssinian woman.

One of my favourite stories of the Prophet ﷺ with respect to this theme actually occurs near the end of his life. Before the commencement of his final illness, the Prophet ﷺ made two noteworthy and memorable trips. The *masjid* is not included in this count, as it is already established that he would attempt to lead the prayer there as much as he could until his health severely deteriorated. The first of these two trips was the Prophet's visit to Mount Uḥud. The purpose of this visit was in order to seek forgiveness and make *duʿā'* for the martyrs (*shuhadā'*) of the fateful battle. His final trip is reported in elaborate detail in a well known narration of the Companion Abū Muwayhibah رضي الله عنه. In it, the Prophet ﷺ is reported to have said: "I have been commanded to seek forgiveness for the people of Baqīʿ." Thus, he proceeded towards the famous graveyard, and asked Allah ﷻ to forgive all the Companions رضي الله عنهم who were buried there.

These final actions are a great testimony to the character of the Prophet ﷺ, and set the best example for anyone who belongs to his Ummah. One cannot fail to notice that the Prophet ﷺ exerted all his efforts in the last stage of his life; he sought forgiveness for his beloved Companions and family members. Through these actions the Prophet ﷺ was imparting an extremely important lesson to all of us. As Muslims and followers of the Prophet ﷺ we should strive to visit our loved ones often and frequently make *duʿā'* for them.

It is common for people to ask whether their deceased loved ones can hear and sense their presence when they visit their gravesite. When answering this question, it is first important to note that the Prophet ﷺ has angels who deliver our greetings (*salām*) directly to him regardless of where we are. This is even if we are extremely distant from his grave in geographical terms, such as being continents away from him. Regardless of where in the globe you are, if you utter the honorific phrase *ṣallallāh ʿalayhi wa sallam*, it will inevitably reach the Prophet ﷺ. This is undoubtedly a special quality which the Prophet ﷺ possesses.

As for the visitation of normal individuals, there are strong indicators that they too hear and perceive our actions in their presence. For instance, when entering the graveyard, it is recommended to make the following *duʿāʾ*, which has slight differences in wording:

السَّلاَمُ عَلَيْكُمْ أَهْلَ الدِّيَارِ مِنَ الْمُؤْمِنِينَ وَالْمُسْلِمِينَ

*"Peace be upon you, O inhabitants of the graves,
from the believers and the Muslims."*

For the first part of the supplication, we are required to give a general greeting to everyone in the graveyard. The next part of the supplication is:

أَنْتُمُ السَّابِقُونَ وَنَحْنُ إِنْ شَاءَ اللَّهُ بِكُمْ لَاحِقُونَ

*"You are the forerunners and have preceded us,
and in shā Allāh we will soon follow you."*

The final part of the supplication reads:

نَسْأَلُ اللَّهَ لَنَا وَلَكُمُ الْعَافِيَةَ

"We ask Allah for well-being for us and for you."

Throughout this invocation, one is directly addressing the inhabitants of the graves with words of greeting after approaching them. Likewise, it is well known that when one visits the grave of the Prophet ﷺ one should directly address the Prophet ﷺ by saying, "Greetings, O Messenger of Allah (*Al-Salam ʿalayka, yā Rasūl Allāh*)." After greeting the Prophet ﷺ, one then proceeds to address Abū Bakr ◌ and ʿUmar ◌ with words of peace as well. For Ibn 'Umar ﷺ, this greeting was done in a slightly different way, because 'Umar ﷺ was his father. He would first approach the Prophet's grave and say:

السَّلَامُ عَلَيْكَ يَا رَسُولَ اللهِ

"Peace be upon you, O Messenger of Allah."

Then he would move over a bit, and say:

السَّلَامُ عَلَيْكَ يَا أَبَا بَكْرٍ

"Peace be upon you, O Abū Bakr."

And then he would move on and say:

السَّلَامُ عَلَيْكَ يَا أَبَتِ

"Peace be upon you, O father."

Ultimately, the children of Abū Bakr and 'Umar ﷺ would have a unique and beautiful experience whenever they passed by the Prophet's grave.

The main issues for this segment include determining what benefits one obtains when going to the graveyard. The second issue is whether or not the dead can actually perceive the presence, identity, and verbal greetings of their visitors. As for the first issue, the permissibility of visiting the graveyards was only legislated in the latter years of the Prophet's life. The Prophet ﷺ alluded to the early ruling of prohibition when he said:

كُنْتُ نَهَيْتُكُمْ عَنْ زِيَارَةِ الْقُبُورِ فَزُورُوهَا فَإِنَّهَا تُذَكِّرُكُمُ الْمَوْتَ

"I used to forbid you from visiting the graves, but now visit them, for they remind you of death."

The Prophet ﷺ even mentioned why one should visit the graves: they remind us of death and the Hereafter. This point is of immense significance, since it indicates that the purpose behind the visit is not to benefit the deceased, but our very own selves. For instance, with regards to the Prophet ﷺ, our greetings reach him wherever he is. While this is unique to him, the point is that one needs not be physically before his grave to communicate greetings to him. But even on a more general note, the *duʿā's* and good deeds one does on behalf of people of faith (*īmān*) benefit them wherever they are done. It is incorrect to believe that *duʿā'* done at the graveyard has more benefits than the *duʿā'* done at one's home. On the contrary, one can confer rewards and benefits to the deceased through the good acts that they perform, regardless of where they are situated. In fact, they are far more in need of that than anything else.

This analysis supports the conclusion that the prohibition of visiting graves was abrogated so that the visitors would be able to spiritually benefit by being reminded of death or the Hereafter. Therefore, the point is not to benefit the occupiers of the gravers themselves. However, there are a few reports which may at first sight give credence to the opposite conclusion. For instance, while on his deathbed, ʿAmr ibn al-ʿĀṣ ﷺ instructed his children to wait by his grave after his burial, so he could be comforted by their presence (*asta'nis bikum*) until the interrogation with the angels would begin. There are other narrations which apparently seem to support the prescription of ʿAmr ibn al-ʿĀṣ ﷺ.

According to these reports, when a believer visits a grave, the male and female inhabitants of the graveyard are comforted by their presence and respond to their greetings (*ista'nas bihim*). Some of these narrations, however, are of disputed authenticity, and the scholars disagree on whether they are acceptable.

In any case, the upshot is that the main purposes of going to the grave include giving greetings to the inhabitants of the grave, making *du'ā'* for them, and reminding oneself of death. While performing these actions, one can be assured that one's good deeds will benefit the deceased, regardless of where they are done.

One can state with sufficient confidence that the dead are not capable of hearing everything happenning in the world of the living. They are not like the living, such that they can roam everywhere and enter someone's room, for instance. Nor do they have access to all the news regarding the affairs of this world (*dunyā*). However, it is established from the Sunnah of the Prophet ﷺ that they can indeed hear some things in their burial place. For instance, in an authentic narration the Prophet ﷺ mentioned that after the conclusion of the funeral (*janāzah*), the deceased can actually hear the footsteps of the last congregants departing from their grave. Likewise, in the aftermath of the Battle of Badr, the Prophet ﷺ addressed the dead disbelievers by saying:

يَا فُلَانَ بْنَ فُلَانٍ وَيَا فُلَانَ بْنَ فُلَانٍ هَلْ وَجَدْتُمْ مَا وَعَدَكُمُ اللَّهُ وَرَسُولُهُ حَقًّا،
فَإِنِّي قَدْ وَجَدْتُ مَا وَعَدَنِي اللَّهُ حَقًّا

"O so and so, the son of so and so! O so and so, the son of so and so! Have you found what Allah and His Messenger promised to be true? For I have certainly found what Allah has promised me to be true."

When the Prophet ﷺ said that, the Companions ﷺ asked him, "O Messenger of Allah! Can they hear what you are saying?" In response, the Prophet ﷺ said: "You cannot hear any better than what they are hearing." Thus, Allah ﷻ certainly caused the disbelievers to hear every single word that the Prophet ﷺ addressed them with.

A number of tentative conclusions can be drawn from this event. Most importantly, the key inference is that the dead can hear whatever Allah ﷻ wishes them to hear. Undoubtedly, the reward of the righteous deeds done on their behalf will reach them, and the benefit of one's *du'ā'* will be transferred to them as well. Furthermore, there is a plethora of primary and secondary evidence which encourages Muslims to go to the graveyard and give greetings to the dead. There is nothing in the Sunnah which indicates that a person should request things from the dead. Neither is there any textual evidence that one should ask the dead to make *du'ā'* for one. Instead, the fundamental point stressed in the Sunnah is that by greeting them the dead will attain some degree of comfort and a special form of spiritual connection with the living. Lastly, their level of comfort will increase when one makes *du'ā'* for them and does good deeds on their behalf.

Peace be upon you, O inhabitants of the graves, from the believers and the Muslims. You are the forerunners and have preceded us, and in shā Allāh, we will soon follow you. We ask Allah for well-being for us and for you.

8

Do They Know What Is Happening to Me?

When a righteous person passes away, not only do we long for their presence, but we also miss the positive influence they used to have on us. For instance, parents or guardians are undoubtedly positive forms of influence vis-à-vis their children by telling them to pray and perform other righteous deeds. However, after they have departed from this world, that beneficial form of influence ceases to exist.

It is often the case that when a righteous person passes away, the grieving family experiences a heightened sense of religiosity. But over time, this heightened sense of spiritual consciousness begins to decline. This often occurs because the household members lose their sense of purpose, and thereby return to their old habits. While they may continue to maintain a relationship and attachment to the dead family member, they do not heed the lessons which this instance of death brought forth; ultimately, they fail to adjust their life patterns accordingly. Episodes of death are supposed to spiritually awaken the living who are heedless and negligent of their religious responsibilities towards their Creator. However, many people who are living are still spiritually asleep, despite breathing and walking around us. Paradoxically, those who have passed away have awakened and perceive a metaphysical reality which many of us ignore.

These realities became most manifest when the Prophet ﷺ passed away. It behooves us to start with his death since his departure from this world undoubtedly left the greatest impact. ʿAbdullāh ibn ʿAmr ibn al-ʿĀṣ ؓ once said: "When we were with the Prophet, it was different. For me to do a good deed now is twice as beloved to me as when the Prophet was with us." The people who heard this said, "Why?" They did not understand why performing a good deed in the presence of the Prophet ﷺ was not better and more beloved to him. ʿAbdullāh ibn ʿAmr ibn al-ʿĀṣ ؓ explained by saying:

لِأَنَّا كُنَّا مَعَ رَسُولِ اللهِ يَهُمُّنَا الآخِرَةُ وَلَا تَهُمُّنَا الدُّنْيَا ، وَإِنَّ الْيَوْمَ مَالَتْ بِنَا الدُّنْيَا

"Because when we were with the Messenger of Allah, all we cared about was the Hereafter, and the world did not concern us. As for today, we are concerned about the world."

With this statement, he indicated that their state of affairs had drastically changed; for that reason, they worried about themselves. Every one of the Companions ؓ of the Prophet ﷺ feared hypocrisy and being considered from the ranks of the hypocrites. This is despite the fact that they were considered to be the best generation of people, and registered the most pious and knowledgeable of individuals. When one of their brothers or sisters died, they worried and asked whether or not they were amongst the righteous.

The root of piety starts with developing a state of consciousness of Allah ﷻ (*taqwā*). This is where one develops the realisation that Allah ﷻ always can see what is inside one's heart, and no one can know more about one than Allah ﷻ. This eventually culminates in the understanding that one should fear no one's sight except the sight of Allah ﷻ. However, you should be greatly concerned about disappointing your relatives and other family members who have departed this world, as they are aware of your current state, and long for you to become righteous and attain salvation. There is in fact a powerful narration from Abū Dardā' ؓ pertaining to this matter. Abū Dardā' ؓ was known to be one of the most knowledgeable and righteous Companions ؓ. But he became even more serious in his religious observance after his brother in Hijrah 'Abdullāh ibn Rawāḥah ؓ passed away. To understand the context of this relation, it is important to note that the Prophet ﷺ paired members of the Emigrants (*Muhājirūn*) with the Helpers (*Anṣār*) in order to increase their solidarity and religious bonds. It so happened that Abū Dardā' ؓ was paired with 'Abdullāh ibn Rawāḥah ؓ, and they treated each other like blood brothers. After the latter passed away, Abū Dardā' ؓ used to make *du'ā'* for him by saying:

اللَّهُمَّ إِنِّي أَعُوذُ بِكَ أَنْ أَعْمَلَ عَمَلًا أَخْزَى بِهِ عِنْدَ عَبْدِ اللهِ بْنِ رَوَاحَةَ

"O Allah, I seek refuge in You from doing something which would disgrace me in the sight of 'Abdullāh ibn Rawāḥah."

The implications of this narration are huge. It indicates that there are conversations between the souls of those who have preceded us. Besides holding conversations about those who have arrived, they will also discuss amongst themselves the state of affairs of those who have been left behind. They will be asking the souls which recently reached them about any news regarding our state of affairs and religiosity. They will inquire whether we are religious and practising. More specifically, they will ask about our quality of worship (*ʿibādah*), such as whether or not we go to the *masjid* in a regular basis. In essence, our forerunners and loved ones who left the world before us will be concerned about our spiritual state. We should be motivated and spurred on to turn back to Allah ﷻ immediately if we know that our name is currently being mentioned in an unfavourable manner among those who preceded us. Some of us may have buried people that we love more than ourselves, such as our mothers, fathers, brothers, sisters, spouses or child. That intense love and connection we hold vis-à-vis that person is what causes us to invoke Allah ﷻ by saying, "O Allah, I do not want my loved one to see me in a way that would shame me in his or her sights."

Anas ibn Mālik ؓ narrates an extremely powerful narration from the Prophet ﷺ, which is recorded in the *Musnad* of Imam Aḥmad ؒ. Shaykh al-Albānī, who is a contemporary *muḥaddith*, initially graded it as weak, but later in his life authenticated it. In this moving narration, the Prophet ﷺ is reported to have said: "The deeds of the living are shown to those who have passed away. If they see good deeds, they are happy and delighted (*istabsharū bihi*)." They rejoice and praise Allah by saying *alḥamdulillāh* for seeing their loved one in a good state. They thank Allah that this person has remained in the same state they left them in. In fact, they may rejoice that their death was the catalyst for leading their living relative to repentance (*tawbah*) and the path towards Allah ﷻ. Ultimately, they are pleased to see their living loved one on the right path, and on the way to joining the rest of the righteous souls. They will be pleased to see their loved one performing good deeds and exercising righteous conduct, and further rejoice upon hearing pleasant news from the new souls that enter the spiritual realm. However, if they see or are informed that their relative is in a spiritually negative state replete with evil deeds, they will be saddened. In response, they will invoke Allah ﷻ by saying:

وَإِنْ كَانَ غَيْرَ ذَلِكَ قَالُوا اللَّهُمَّ لَا تُمِتْهُمْ حَتَّى تَهْدِيَهُمْ كَمَا هَدَيْتَنَا

"If they see evil, they will say: 'O Allah, do not cause them to die until You guide them like You guided us.'"

If you are in a spiritually deficient state, your deceased loved ones will be concerned about you, in a way commensurate with how you care about them and send good deeds on their behalf. Even if your religious commitment is lacking, you nevertheless share and feel a connection with them. Likewise, they are always concerned about you and want to see you obtain salvation in the Hereafter. They have access to a metaphysical reality where good deeds can be seen and identified. Their ultimate desire is to hear about your righteous deeds and your good standing. Abū Ayyūb al-Anṣārī ؓ once said: "The deeds of the living are shown to the dead. If they receive good news, they become pleased. If they see that which is evil, they supplicate to Allah by saying:

اللَّهُمَّ رَاجِعْ بِعَبْدِكَ

'O Allah, turn Your servant away from this evil!'"

There are numerous narrations which support and establish the same theme. What seems to be the case is that the individuals who pass away between us and our loved ones transfer news regarding our spiritual and religious state. Allah ﷻ knows best what other secrets and astonishing metaphysical realties exist in that other realm. The key point is that just as we maintain a sense of Allah's observance (*murāqabah*) over us and we seek to preserve a connection with the dead by doing good deeds for them, we must not forget our own state as well. We must ensure that we perform a sufficient amount of good deeds so we can join them in the pleasant place we believe they are currently in.

9

What If I Dream About Them?

Many of the most powerful and moving dreams that people witness in their lives involve a deceased loved one. Oftentimes, these dreams possess powerful themes and messages to the extent that the person who sees them becomes alarmed. The existence of these types of dreams yields two main questions. First and foremost, is there a way one can come to terms with these visions and images which ones sees during one's sleep? Secondly, are we actually witnessing the souls of our loved ones when we see such visions?

There are many incidents pertaining to dreams during the Prophet's time which one can relate, a fact which makes choosing one to focus on a difficult endeavour. But there is one particularly fascinating episode which involved Ṭufayl ibn ʿAmr al-Dawsī ﷺ, which is worth starting with for this discussion. Ṭufayl ibn ʿAmr ﷺ was known to have a number of notable interactions with the Prophet ﷺ. He played a decisive role in ensuring that the tribe of Daws embraced Islam and accepted the Prophet's call. Another noteworthy fact about Ṭufayl ؓ is that he was one of the Companions ؓ who made Hijrah to the city of Madinah. When he embarked upon his journey, he had a fellow tribe member accompany him to Madinah. This man left everything that he owned and possessed behind so he could come to the city of Madinah. Unfortunately, the climate in Madinah did not suit him; he became severely ill and suffered. His pain eventually became so intense that he started cutting off his fingers. When he did so, he began to bleed intensely, and eventually passed away.

What happened next was extremely fascinating. Ṭufayl ؓ stated: "I saw him in a dream, where he was in a good state." This was a positive sign that he was from among the people of Paradise. At the same time, however, his hands were heavily wrapped, which indicated that his fingers were not restored, but still cut off. As a result, Ṭufayl ؓ asked him: "What has Allah done with you?" The man responded with the following answer: "Allah pardoned me as a result of my Hijrah with the Prophet. But as for my fingers, Allah said to me: 'I will not restore what you yourself have ruined. I will not restore what you yourself ruined.'"

At this point, Ṭufayl ؓ relates that the Prophet ﷺ raised his hands to the sky and said:

اللَّهُمَّ وَلِيَدَيْهِ فَاغْفِرْ، اللَّهُمَّ وَلِيَدَيْهِ فَاغْفِرْ

"O Allah, and for his hands forgive him.
O Allah, and for his hands forgive him."

Numerous dreams of a similar nature have been narrated. This is not just in the case of the Prophet ﷺ and his Companions ﵃, but even later episodes in Muslim history. For instance, it is common for students to see their teachers during their sleep. At this juncture, specific focus will be given to a narration of the noble Companion ʿUthmān ﵁, where he saw the Prophet ﷺ in a dream. Before mentioning the narration in question, it is first worth mentioning that ʿUthmān ﵁ was known for his immense fear of the trials of the grave. It is indeed a difficult endeavour to find another Companion that matches this immense level of fearfulness of what would happen after one is buried. As a result, it is no surprise to find narrations which mention that ʿUthmān ﵁ used to often cry at graves. In fact, it is reported that he wept so much that his beard would become wet. Yet, most interestingly, he would not weep in that manner whenever Paradise or Hellfire were mentioned in his presence. Subsequently, he was asked to explain why he feared the grave more than anything else. In response, he stated: "This is the first station of the stations of the Hereafter." By this, he meant that if everything in the grave went well, a person's path to Paradise would be ensured. However, if he faced torment and punishment in the grave, his salvation would be in serious jeopardy.

With these background points now explained in full, the actual story can be related, which occurred when ʿUthmān ﵁ was about to die. Near the end of his life, ʿUthmān ﵁ was under siege. While in this state, he once went to sleep while fasting. It was at this point that he saw a vivid dream that the Prophet, Abū Bakr ﵁, and ʿUmar ﵁ were before him. The Prophet ﷺ

comforted ʿUthmān ؓ for the trials he was currently experiencing. Then the Prophet ﷺ told him the following:

اِرْجِعْ فَإِنَّكَ مُفْطِرٌ عِنْدِي

"Go back, for you will be breaking your fast with me."

Through this message, the Prophet ﷺ informed ʿUthmān ؓ that he would be celebrating the end of his fast (*ifṭār*) with him, Abū Bakr, and ʿUmar ؓ. After waking up from this moving dream, ʿUthmān ؓ was delighted and began to laugh. He then firmly stated:

وَلَنْ تَغِيبَ الشَّمْسُ هَذَا الْيَوْمَ، وَاللهِ إِلَّا وَأَنَا مِنْ أَهْلِ الْآخِرَةِ

"The Sun will not set on this day except that I will be from the people of the Hereafter."

He then grabbed his *muṣḥaf*, and continued reading from it until he was assassinated. So on that very day he did in fact break his fast with the Prophet ﷺ, Abū Bakr, and ʿUmar ؓ, just as he was informed in his dream.

There are several narrations to this effect, many of which are narrated in works like *Madārij al-Sālikīn* and *Iḥyā' ʿUlūm al-Dīn*. In several of these transmitted stories, students relate how they saw their teachers in a state of bliss in Paradise. In one of these stories, a student asked his teacher regarding how he were able to find salvation. In response, the teacher said: "Allah did not accept anything from me except for two *rakʿahs* that I prayed in the nights." This is in fact a form of sincere advice (*naṣīḥah*) which teachers were imparting to their students, as they were indicating to them how they should orient themselves in the world.

The next topic pertains to the reality and metaphysical nature of dreams, and whether through them we actually see and interact with our loved ones. First and foremost, it is important to note that bad dreams come from the *Shayṭān*. Whenever we see and experience such dreams, we are to seek refuge in Allah ﷻ from them and not entertain others with their content. Thus, whenever you see a dream that bothers and discomforts you, say:

أَعُوذُ بِاللهِ مِنَ الشَّيْطَانِ الرَّجِيمِ

"I seek refuge in Allah from the accursed Shayṭān."

The simple course of action in such a scenario is to seek refuge in Allah ﷻ and to avoid seeking the interpretation of the dream. As for good dreams where one sees one's dead loved ones, it is possible that one is merely experiencing regurgitated thoughts (*ḥadīth al-nafs*). At the same time, however, the possibility of actually seeing a dead loved one in one's sleep is something which the scholars of Islam confirm. Ibn al-Qayyim ؒ has described this phenomenon by stating that the soul is able to freely move during the time of sleep. When Allah ﷻ compared sleep to death (*mawt*), He was actually alluding to the fact that sleep is a minor form of death. Every time a person goes to sleep, he or she recites the following invocation:

بِاسْمِكَ اللَّهُمَّ أَمُوتُ وَأَحْيَا

"In Your name, O Allah, I die and am given life."

Likewise, after a person wakes up from sleep, he or she recites the following:

الحَمْدُ لِلَّهِ الَّذِي أَحْيَانَا بَعْدَمَا أَمَاتَنَا وَإِلَيْهِ النُّشُورُ

"All praise be to the One Who gave us life after He took our souls, and unto Him is the resurrection."

This ultimately means that every night one goes to sleep, one experiences death and one's soul travels. The soul is able to freely move during sleep, and even meets other souls as well. Because of these factors, Ibn al-Qayyim ﵀ argued that it is possible for one's soul to meet a deceased loved one during sleep. It is important to note in this context that a person is not limited to the dimensions of this world while sleeping. It then becomes possible for one's soul to meet with a dead person; the latter may comfort one, give assurances of his or her well-being, show his or her place in Paradise, and impart words of sincere advice. Overall, the soul of the dead will comfort the living family member with soothing words. It might even be the case that the soul will remind the living member of a debt he or she never had the chance to repay, and ask him or her to settle it as soon as possible. As discussed in an earlier segment, this is one of the first things that the relatives and heirs must do once a person passes away: pay off any outstanding debts. It has even been the case that during some dreams the soul of the dead requests the living family member to ask a person they had wronged to forgive them.

A few years ago, one of my own family members passed away while performing Hajj. This apparently seemed like a good sign, as dying while performing Hajj is considered to be a type of martyrdom (*shahādah*). However, a short time after his passing, all of his children saw the same dream: the deceased was requesting them to seek forgiveness from a particular person. The next day, they found out that every one of them had seen the same vision. They followed the order of their father's soul and went to that particular person, seeking his forgiveness on their father's behalf. Afterwards, they saw their father in another dream, but this time he was in Paradise. The vivid contrast between the two dreams indicated that hurting or harming a person can prevent even the most righteous of people who dies in an ideal manner from reaching their desired place with Allah ﷻ. This story reveals a number of valuable insights. It indicates that our loved ones may appear to us during our dreams and order us to correct certain wrongs that they committed during their lives. Such events have been confirmed to have occurred with countless individuals. In other cases, they appear during sleep to remind their loved ones of the Hereafter and preparing for it with good deeds.

However, with reference to dreams, one cannot accept any imperatives or orders which are forbidden or go contrary to the rulings of Islam. Such dreams are most certainly from the accursed *Shayṭān*, and should be disregarded. It should be noted that as an exception the *Shayṭān* cannot imitate or impersonate the Prophet ﷺ in any circumstances whatsoever. This means that one be assured that if one sees or converses with the Prophet, then one has indeed seen him, as his form cannot be assumed by anyone else. On this matter, the Prophet said: "Whoever sees me in a dream, then no doubt he has seen me, for the *Shayṭān* cannot take my form."

As a final point, it should be mentioned that one should not adopt the opposite extreme by believing that seeing dreams is a barometer of piety and righteousness. Simply put, a person should not be concerned if he or she never sees his or her loved ones in dreams. Unfortunately, it is common to find individuals holding erroneous beliefs simply because they do not see their dead family members in their sleep. They often believe that something may be wrong with them in their religiosity and piety which prevents them from visiting the souls of the other world. Or they may suppose that their deceased relatives are angry with them, since they never enjoyed the opportunity to see and converse with them in their sleep. In fact, some go as far as assuming that Allah must be displeased with them. None of these beliefs are accurate in any way whatsoever. This is because many of the individuals who were most beloved to Allah ﷻ and closely followed the Sunnah never saw the Prophet ﷺ in a dream. The absence of any such dreams does not diminish their status, observance of the Sunnah, or good deeds. Instead, the opportunity to see the Prophet ﷺ and other righteous people in a dream is a blessing that Allah chooses to give to some of His slaves. While we may not know the criteria for how one qualifies for such a blessing, we are certain that His choice has a hidden wisdom (*ḥikmah*) which He Himself knows. While it is true that every person aspires to see the souls of their dead loved ones, a person should not fear that he or she are cursed or wicked if his or her wishes do not come true. Righteousness and wickedness should only be evaluated and measured through the standards set by Allah ﷻ Himself. Such standards have no bearing or relation to seeing one's friends or relatives in dreams.

10

Are They Considered Shuhadā'?

"I need to know where my son is. Is he in Paradise? Did he make it or not?"

There was a young man by the name of Ḥārithah ibn Surāqah ﷺ who had a close connection with his mother. On the day of the Battle of Badr, he joined ranks with the Prophet ﷺ, and was ultimately hit by a stray arrow. He passed away as a result of his injury. After his mother found out that he had died, she approached the Prophet ﷺ and addressed him by saying:

يَا رَسُولَ اللهِ أَخْبِرْنِي عَنْ حَارِثَةَ، فَإِنْ كَانَ فِي الجَنَّةِ صَبَرْتُ وَإِنْ كَانَ غَيْرَ ذَلِكَ اِجْتَهَدْتُ عَلَيْهِ فِي البُكَاءِ

"O Messenger of Allah, inform me of what happened to Ḥārithah. If he is in Paradise, then I will be patient. But if he is not in Paradise, then I will continue exerting myself in crying over his loss."

The Prophet ﷺ responded to her question by mentioning that Paradise is not one indivisible entity, but instead consists of multiple levels. He then mentioned that her son had in fact reached the highest level of Paradise (*Jannah al-Firdaws*).

When someone passes away, it is sometimes the case that the living family members and friends ask whether the deceased died as a martyr (*shahīd*). As Muslims, we are aware of the different stations of death, and realise the uppermost rank that the status of martyrdom occupies. Everyone wishes to know with certainty that their deceased loved one has been blessed with this rank, so that they could be content that the door of Paradise has been opened for him or her. It is for this reason that many living family members wish that they could see a dream where they find their deceased loved one in Paradise. Of course, a person who has died as a martyr or a believer wishes that he or she could find a way to return to their families and inform them of their salvation. But unfortunately, such transfer of information is not possible.

There are different categories of martyrs in Islam. Obviously, the main and highest form of martyrdom is being killed in the battlefield. A martyr who dies in battle is given a number of unique legal rulings (*aḥkām*) which relate to the rituals—such as shrouding and prayer—that should be performed for them. Only this form of martyrdom has these specific rulings.

However, the Prophet ﷺ indicated in a number of narrations that the station of martyrdom is also conferred to other categories as well. One of these categories is the person who dies due to a plague. Being aware of this category is extremely crucial, especially since we find ourselves in the time of the COVID-19 pandemic. We pray to Allah ﷻ that He accepts all of the people who died due to COVID-19 in a state of faith (*īmān*) as martyrs. By the permission of Allah, they appear to match the definition of the person who dies due to plague.

In a *ḥadīth*, the Prophet ﷺ mentioned that the person who dies as a result of drowning is also a martyr. In addition, he mentioned that the person who dies due to a fire is given this special rank. A person who leaves this world due to pleurisy is also given this honourable station. People who die as a result of stomach or intestinal disease are likewise considered martyrs. However, one should be aware that the terms which the Prophet ﷺ used for these categories are much more open-ended than the specific meanings which these words may impart in a contemporary medical sense. These designations ultimately do not carry the specific meanings that they may have today. As a result, the words used for translating the Prophet's words may be too specific, in fact. For instance, instead of simply saying that people who die due to pleurisy or inflammation of the lungs are considered martyrs, it would in fact be more accurate to confer the same rank to people who die due to chest pains and heart attacks as well. In a parallel fashion, for the other category it would be reductionist to say that only people who die due to a stomach disease are considered martyrs. Instead, it would be more accurate to state that this category encompasses any person who dies in an untimely manner due to an internal illness, such as cancer.

Another category of martyrdom is the woman who dies in childbirth, regardless of whether she dies while being pregnant, giving birth, or nursing her newborn child. The reason why she is conferred this special rank is because during the pregnancy and delivery process she finds herself in a state of struggle (*jihād*). During this time, she exposes herself to serious risk and danger, yet still persists. Thus, if she passes away during this period, which does occur occasionally, she is considered a martyr due to her strength and bravery. The Prophet ﷺ also mentioned that the person who dies while defending his property is considered a martyr. This shows that a person is not rewarded just for protecting Allah's religion, but he or she is are elevated in rank when he or she dies as a result of protecting his or her own possessions. One could only imagine how immense the rewards would be if someone dies in an attempt to protect someone else's life or property.

A related but different category is the person who dies while defending their lives or family. If someone is killed—may Allah ﷻ protect us and our loved ones—while trying to protect his family members, then he is blessed with the eminent rank of martyrdom. Furthermore, the Prophet ﷺ mentioned that the person who is crushed by a falling structure (*ṣāḥib al-hadm*) is considered a martyr. Many contemporary scholars consider a person who dies in a car accident to fall under the remit of this category, since automobiles did not exist back then. But because a person killed in a car accident oftentimes is impacted just like a person who has a structure fall on him, the scholars annexed the former new case to the original. All of these scenarios are considered to be forms of martyrdom, and their underlying theme is the occurrence of an unexpected death.

The Prophet ﷺ told us to always have good expectations (*ḥusn al-ẓann*) of Allah ﷻ. Thus, it follows that if someone dies shortly after facing one of the above diseases or disasters, then we should—despite lacking certainty—have the good expectation from Allah ﷻ that he or she will be considered a martyr. However, once a person dies in one of the aforementioned ways, the living friends and family members may be troubled by the state of his or her body and how he or she has changed. This theme was already explored when the martyrs of Uḥud (*shuhadā' Uḥud*) were discussed. A person may come across a dead body which has been mutilated or severely damaged due to a car accident, and immediately say in shock, "*Subḥānallāh*, what has happened to that person?" Regarding this sensitive matter, one must keep in mind that the soul transcends the body. This is in fact why the Prophet ﷺ said:

يُغْفَرُ لَهُ فِي أَوَّلِ دُفْعَةٍ مِنْ دَمِهِ، وَيَرَى مَقْعَدَهُ مِنَ الجَنَّةِ

"The person is forgiven at the first strike, and shown their place in Paradise."

These truths can be exemplified in the story of Āsiyah. She was killed in a horrific way, yet she exemplified perfect and pristine faith. She is likewise an epitome of martyrdom, as she stood up to the tyranny of Firʿawn until the last moment of her life. Allah saved her before the stone fell on top of her. Ultimately, as Muslims we should not be worried about the condition of the deceased body when we know that the soul of the martyr

has been promised with so much goodness.
A person may wonder whether he or she can also die as a martyr. As Muslims, it is crucial that we make *du'ā'* for attaining the reward of martyrdom. Allah does not actually need us to fall into a certain state in order for us to obtain a certain station. If we demonstrate sincerity and ask Allah ﷻ genuinely for the reward of martyrdom, we can obtain that station. There is a beautiful *ḥadīth* from the Prophet ﷺ, where he said:

مَنْ سَأَلَ اللهَ الشَّهَادَةَ صَادِقًا بَلَّغَهُ اللهُ مَنَازِلَ الشُّهَدَاءِ، وَإِنْ مَاتَ عَلَى فِرَاشِهِ

"Whoever asks Allah for martyrdom with truthfulness in his heart, Allah will give him the station of martyrdom, even if they die on their bed."

Truthfulness (*ṣidq*) in one's heart is the key variable which allows one to realise the elevated ranks of the martyrs (*manāzil al-shuhadā'*). The outcome does not matter, such that it would be required for one's body to be desecrated or mutilated. Such a station can even be obtained while someone is on his or her bed. We hope and pray that Allah ﷻ grants us and our relatives the rank of martyrdom without actually having to be from the categories mentioned above.

11

Losing a Child

During the divine night journey (*al-Isrā' wa al-Mi'rāj*), the Prophet ﷺ related that one of the most prominent scenes he encountered was a beautiful garden which contained every conceivable colour. He then said that he noticed an extremely tall man inside the garden. He was so tall that his head actually reached above the clouds. The Prophet ﷺ observed that there were children playing around this man. Interestingly, the Prophet ﷺ also remarked that he had never seen so many children in one place. To appreciate this scenery, imagine being situated in a most beautiful garden, where you observe a man who is so tall that his head is in the sky. In addition, you find children rejoicing and playing in every segment of this garden. The Prophet turned to the angels accompanying him in his journey, and said: "Who is this man?" In response, the angels said: "This is Ibrāhīm ﷺ." Then the Prophet ﷺ asked about the identities of the children playing around him. The angels said in response: "These are the children who died in a state of original purity (*fiṭrah*)." One of the Companions ﷺ who was listening to these accounts of the divine night journey then said: "O Messenger of Allah, what about the children of the disbelievers?" The Prophet ﷺ said in response: "And the children of the disbelievers."

Ultimately, this account demonstrates that when a prepubescent child dies, there is no uncertainty and ambiguity about their destination in the Hereafter. Nevertheless, the greater issue of concern is the pain that parents feel once they lose their child. In fact, that is likely to be one of the most difficult trials that they can face in their life. A parent is always willing to sacrifice his or her own wealth and health instead of seeing their child suffer or perish. Taking these factors into mind, there is no doubt that it is a nightmare for a parent to lose a child. There are many *ḥadīth*s from the Prophet ﷺ which reflect these themes and the severity of this trial. For instance, in one key *ḥadīth*, the Prophet ﷺ mentioned that after the death of a child, Allah ﷻ asks the angels: "Did you take the coolness of the eyes of My servant?" They will say in response: "Yes, O Allah." Then, with reference to the grief of the parent, Allah ﷻ asks: "And what did my servant say as a result of that?" The angels respond by saying:

حَمِدَكَ وَاسْتَرْجَعَ

"He praised You (ḥamidaka) and said, 'To Allah we belong, and to Him we return.'"

Allah will then say to the angels:

اِبْنُوا لِعَبْدِي بَيْتًا فِي الجَنَّةِ، وَسَمُّوهُ بَيْتَ الحَمْدِ

"Build for My servant a house in Paradise, and name that house the House of Praise."

Because this parent persevered with this unique tragedy, Allah will provide him a special home in Paradise. The Prophet ﷺ himself was well aware of the pain and grief this tragedy brought forth, since he had to bury six out of his seven children. We know a great deal about the last child he lost, because he was born in Madinah after the beginning of the Islamic mission. When the Prophet's son Ibrāhīm was ill and nearing the end of his life, the Companions رضي الله عنهم were with the Prophet ﷺ and observed the grief he was going through. When Ibrāhīm was close to dying, the Prophet ﷺ entered the room he was in and began to kiss and smell him (*fa qabbalahu wa shammahu*). This is the greatest manifestation of love that a parent can display towards his child. When Ibrāhīm breathed his last, the Prophet ﷺ began to cry. At that point, ʿAbd al-Raḥmān ibn ʿAwf رضي الله عنه looked at the Prophet ﷺ and said:

وَأَنْتَ يَا رَسُولَ اللهِ

"You too, O Messenger of Allah?"

This question is worthy of being analysed in depth. We know for a fact that the Prophet ﷺ has already seen Paradise. He knows that the young children who die prematurely will go to that amazing and lush garden, while being in the company of the Prophet Ibrāhīm عليه السلام. Thus, the Prophet ﷺ knew that his son was in a better place. Ibn ʿAwf ﵁ was thus surprised to see the Prophet ﷺ weep despite these realities. By posing his question, it was as if he was suggesting that this emotional response reflected a lack of contentment (*riḍā*) with the decree of Allah ﷻ. To this objection, the Prophet ﷺ responded by saying:

إِنَّ العَيْنَ لَتَدْمَعُ وَإِنَّ القَلْبَ لَيَحْزَنُ وَإِنَّا عَلَى فِرَاقِكَ يَا إِبْرَاهِيمُ لَمَحْزُونُونَ

"Verily, the eye tears, the heart grieves, and we are saddened over your departure, O Ibrāhīm."

Despite intensely grieving over his departure, the Prophet ﷺ ensured this mourning was in accordance with the divinely set religious limits. For this reason, he added:

وَلَا نَقُولُ إِلَّا مَا يُرْضِي رَبَّنَا

"But we do not say except that which is pleasing to our Lord."

This means that he restricted himself to the expressions of *ḥamd* and *istirjāʿ*, which are activated by saying *alḥamdulillāh* and *innā lillāhi wa innā ilayhi rājiʿūn*. Through these statements one ultimately attains the House of Praise. One does not secure this House by crying less or feeling less sadness. Instead, one is granted this special form of residence by praising Allah ﷻ despite undergoing intense pain. In an important *ḥadīth qudsī*, Allah ﷻ says:

مَا لِعَبْدِي المُؤْمِنِ عِنْدِي جَزَاءٌ إِذَا قَبَضْتُ صَفِيَّهُ مِنْ أَهْلِ الدُّنْيَا ثُمَّ احْتَسَبَهُ إِلَّا الجَنَّةَ

"My servant does not attain a reward with Me except Paradise if I take their chosen one (ṣafī) from this world, if they are patient."

This narration is extremely powerful in both its wording and meaning. The word *ṣafī* and its cognates are used to denote the special choosing of someone or something. For instance, Maryam ﷺ was told by the angels:

إِنَّ اللَّهَ اصْطَفَاكِ

"Surely Allah has selected (iṣṭafāki) you..."[3]

In another verse, Allah ﷻ said:

إِنَّ اللَّهَ اصْطَفَىٰ آدَمَ

"Indeed, Allah chose (iṣṭafā) Ādam..."[4]

In fact, the Prophet ﷺ referred to Ibrāhīm as being his chosen and loved one (*ṣafī*).

There is a similar *ḥadīth* which shares almost the same wording as the one quoted earlier, but instead of discussing the loss of a child, it addresses the person who loses his or her eyesight. There is a latent but significant connection between the loss of children and eyesight, since as an expression we often consider a child as being the coolness or apple of our eyes. Regarding the loss of the first, Allah ﷻ is reported to have said in a *ḥadīth qudsī*: "No one is patient when I take away the apple of his eye and he continues to seek reward from me except that I grant him Paradise." In another *ḥadīth* with an extremely similar wording, Allah ﷻ said: "My servant is not patient with me and seeks

3 *Āl 'Imran*, 42.

4 *Āl 'Imran*, 33.

reward from me when I take away his eyesight except that I will give him Paradise."

Ultimately, all of this implies that the destiny of any child is not the issue in contention. Instead, an issue which bothers parents is whether they will ever be reunited with their child, and if so, whether the latter will remember them again. There are several *ḥadīth*s which address these pivotal themes. For instance, in a significant narration, the Prophet ﷺ is reported to have said: "Any woman who loses three of her children, they will be a shield for her from the Fire." The attendees then said to the Prophet ﷺ: "What about two?" In response, the Prophet ﷺ said: "Even two." This means that any children who are lost in this world will be a shield in the Hereafter, and protect one from any punishment. This correlates well with another *ḥadīth* from the Prophet ﷺ, where he is reported to have said that whoever raises two daughters (*rabbā ṭiflatayn*) and was dedicated to raising them properly (*wa aḥsana tarbiyatahumā*), then Allah will cause them to become a shield from the Fire. Ultimately, this means that even though these children have died and passed on to the next world, they will be a source of safety and salvation for their parents.

There is another narration from Abū Ḥassān, who once asked Abū Hurayrah ﵁: "Two of my sons have died. Can you narrate to me a *ḥadīth* ﵁ from the Messenger of Allah that would help give me some contentment?" Abū Hurayrah ﵁ said: "Yes. These little ones are the little ones of Paradise." He then reported that the Prophet ﷺ said: "When one of them meets his father or his parents on the Day of Judgement, he takes hold of his garment, as I am doing now"—Abū Hurayrah ﵁ demonstrated this tugging with his hand—"and does not let go of his parents until Allah enters them into Paradise." In another narration, the Prophet mentioned something similar, but this time highlighting the intervention that will even be done by the miscarried foetus. Through its umbilical cord, it will help pull its parents to Paradise.

Thus, a deceased child offers its parents both protection from the Fire and entrance into Paradise. What is amazing is that it will be waiting for its parents at the gate of Paradise, to ensure that they will be immediately put inside it. Customarily, it is the case that parents dream to see their children reach adulthood and witness their achievements in the different stages of life, such as graduation, marriage, and other forms of success. Yet, despite dying in an extremely young age, this child will not forget its parents. This is fascinating, since it is often the case that children forget their childhood with the passage of time. This will not be the case with this deceased child in the Hereafter. It will wait for its parents at the gate of Paradise and will not be pleased until both of its parents enter alongside with it. Allah ﷻ has indeed guaranteed young children automatic admission into Paradise, as they did not even live long enough to commit a single sin on Earth.

The Prophet ﷺ himself was well aware of the pain and grief of parents who lose their children. He had to bury six out of his seven children during his lifetime.

12

Condolences

When reflecting back on your hardest moments and the people around you during times of tragedy, you will likely recall many of the insensitive and inconsiderate comments that were made around you. When it comes to positive interactions, you are less likely to remember the good words that were said to you. Instead, you are more likely to remember the good presence of people and the comfort they brought to you.

When someone tells you something inappropriate or out of place, you are likely going to preserve that experience in your memory. There may be some exceptions to that, however.

Ibn ʿAbbās ﷺ narrated that when his father ʿAbbās ﷺ passed away, a Bedouin man approached him to offer condolences. While the words he uttered were simple, they were extremely profound and meaningful. The words were:

خَيْرٌ مِنَ العَبَّاسِ أَجْرُكِ بَعْدَهُ، وَاللهُ خَيْرٌ مِنْكِ لِلعَبَّاسِ

"What is better for you than having your father with you is the reward that Allah gives you for being patient with losing him. And Allah is better for you than your father."

By this concise statement, the Bedouin meant to say that as much as Ibn 'Abbās ۞ loved his father, he should know that the reward for grieving over him properly and being patient with his loss is greater than actually having him present here. Furthermore, in the last part of his statement he indicated that Allah's love and care of 'Abbās ۞ in the next realm amongst the righteous will be far greater than any love and attention Ibn 'Abbās ۞ could give in this world.

This is a short yet comprehensive statement, and in fact fully corresponds with what the Prophet ﷺ taught us to say when offering condolences to people. The Prophet ﷺ would say the following to the grieving family:

إِنَّ لِلَّهِ مَا أَخَذَ وَلَهُ مَا أَعْطَى

"To Allah belongs that which He has taken, and that which He has given."

One observes how in this statement the Prophet ﷺ first mentioned that which Allah ۞ takes, not that which He gives. By this short sentence, the Prophet ﷺ was indicating that a person's loved one never belonged to him or her; all of us belong to Allah ۞. The Prophet ﷺ would then continue by saying:

وَكُلُّ شَيْءٍ عِنْدَهُ بِأَجَلٍ مُسَمًّى

"And everything is with Allah in accordance with its prescribed time."

By this statement, the Prophet ﷺ meant that every single person or thing has his or its expiration date precisely set by Allah ﷻ. Everyone has their prescribed term set on this Earth. Once that term finishes, Allah ﷻ will take that person back, regardless of the circumstances. The final part of the Prophet's statement is:

فَلْتَصْبِرْ وَلْتَحْتَسِبْ

"So be patient and seek reward [from Allah]."

As an alternative supplication the Prophet ﷺ used to say:

عَظَّمَ اللهُ أَجْرَكَ

"May Allah magnify your reward."

In addition, it is reported that he would also add the following sentence to the previous statement when addressing the families of the deceased:

وَأَحْسَنَ اللهُ عَزَاكُمْ وَغَفَرَ اللهُ لِمَيِّتِكُمْ

"And may Allah perfect your grieving and forgive your dead."

These are the words to be used when condolences are expressed to the family of the deceased. However, it is unfortunate to find that during the process of giving condolences (*al-'azā'*), many Muslims fall into practices which are baseless and not sanctioned by the religion. In fact, some of them even oppose the Prophetic Sunnah.

To illustrate the correct normative teachings found in the Sunnah, one may consider what the Prophet ﷺ did after his cousin Jaʿfar ibn Abī Ṭālib ؓ died. In this narration, we are informed how the Prophet had to go to Jaʿfar's residence and inform his family members of his death. In her long and powerful account, Asmā' ؓ mentioned how on that day, she had prepared herself and her children, expecting Jaʿfar ؓ to return. However, much to her surprise, it was the Prophet ﷺ who entered. The Prophet ﷺ called for the children, who ran and jumped with joy. They intensely loved the Prophet ﷺ, as he was not only the Messenger of Allah for them, but also their uncle. The Prophet ﷺ began to embrace, smell, and kiss them. At this point, Asmā' ؓ became alarmed and sensed that something was wrong with the demeanour of the Prophet ﷺ. But she was afraid to actually ask what had happened. Finally, the Prophet ﷺ revealed what was wrong: Jaʿfar ؓ had been martyred. After hearing this devastating news, Asmā' bint ʿUmays ؓ and her children were overtaken with pain. The Prophet ﷺ realised this, and for that reason he said:

$$\text{اِصْنَعُوا لِآلِ جَعْفَرَ طَعَامًا فَقَدْ أَتَاهُمْ مَا يُشْغِلُهُمْ}$$

"Prepare food for the family of Jaʿfar, for they have been afflicted with that which preoccupies them."

By this statement, the Prophet ﷺ meant that the household of Jaʿfar ؓ had become so preoccupied with his death that they could not take care of their own affairs. For this reason, he asked other members of the community to prepare food for them, so they could be freed from some of their commitments and obligations.

Unfortunately, the problem is that in contemporary times, Muslims have completely opposed the Sunnah in this important matter. The Prophet's Sunnah advises people to give the grieving family space. The afflicted family members which are affected by the tragedy can and should have the prerogative to inform others that they need time and space alone so they may grieve without outside disturbance. Unfortunately, it is common to find in the present-day practices people congregating inside the house of the deceased person for the first three days, often between the Maghrib and 'Ishā' prayers. Then, after the 'Ishā' prayer the guests expect to be served food. The attendees engage in frivolous talk and create an unnecessary burden for the grieving family, who then have to serve all these guests and clean up after them. It is unfortunate to even find many of these attendees crowding and making insensitive remarks regarding the deceased. They fail to ponder over the nearness of death, and instead engage in meaningless conversations which pertain to this world (*dunyā*).

There is no doubt that these actions contravene the Prophetic Sunnah. What is actually required of us from a religious standpoint is to undertake actions which will help relieve the pain of the grieving family as much as possible. Instead of forcing them to hold these gatherings and making them serve food for all the attendees, the right course of action is to make food for them through independent initiatives. Even when offering condolences, ensure that you present them in a manner which does not infringe upon the space of the family. If you are a family member of the deceased, consider setting clear and decisive boundaries so that outsiders will respect and uphold your wishes.

With regards to the issue of condolences, there are some narrations from the Companions ﷺ which indicate that they used to consider the convening of gatherings and feasting as being blameworthy forms of mourning (*niyāḥah*) which actually harm the deceased. The golden rule for this matter is that one should always respect the space and boundaries of the grieving family by not being a burden on them. As Muslims, we should take care of the needs of the grieving family as much as we can. Likewise, we should offer condolences without troubling the household by seeking their food and time. The family of the deceased must be kept comfortable at all times; they should not be inconvenienced by traditions which are incorrectly considered as being from the Prophetic Sunnah. The custom of holding formal gatherings in the family's house for three days and nights is a baseless practice. Even worse is when families are expected to be lavish with the type of food that they prepare. This means that the family will have to take care of additional financial expenses as well. They accept these sacrifices by incorrectly believing that this will honour the dead and give them more rewards. Unfortunately, there is nothing in the Sunnah which supports such a conclusion. In fact, many of the scholars have mentioned that condolences should be provided inside the *masjid* and similar settings, such that the family is not overburdened or has its rights infringed upon.

The family itself should decide whether they would like guests or friends to come visit them. If they have no problem with individuals coming over at their house, then there is no harm in that. It is not prohibited for the family to host people during the first three days after a person's death. But they should be entitled to choose who they would like to come for that period, so they will not be burdened with guests and attendees. During this difficult time of giving condolences, the Sunnah seeks to bring ease and comfort for the family. Unfortunately, newly introduced innovations have brought a number of difficulties and harms, which is why the two must be carefully distinguished.

The family must be allowed to grieve for three days in a relaxed environment which is free of burdens. That way, they can effectively reflect and remember Allah ﷻ properly, with the community helping to take care of any burdens. Unfortunately, it is common that the extended family puts pressure on the immediate family and forces the latter to host gatherings and prepare meals for numerous guests. Instead of engaging in such frivolous activities, the entire family unit should grieve together by reciting the Qur'ān, remembering Allah ﷻ, and mentioning the good qualities of the deceased. Reminding one another of death and the Hereafter is also fully appropriate. What is incorrect, however, is to organise extravagant feasts and gatherings which do not honour the dead or the Sunnah of the Prophet ﷺ.

The Prophet's ﷺ Sunnah advises people to give the grieving family space. They must be kept comfortable at all times. We should offer condolences without troubling the household by seeking their food and time. They should not be inconvenienced in any way while they are grieving.

13

The Widow

Upon observing the Prophetic *sīrah* specifically and Islamic history generally, we often feel much pride when we observe how much our pious ancestors took care of widowed women. As soon as the waiting period (*'iddah*) of these women finished, they received marriage proposals from a long list of men who aspired to take care of them and their families. Unfortunately, it seems as if the present is completely detached from our honourable and golden history; everything has now just been relegated to the realm of marriage. That is without any doubt a huge loss which we must aim to address.

Before discussing the mourning period and the legal rulings pertaining to it, it is imperative to first discuss the forgotten Sunnah of caring for the widow. Unfortunately, this Sunnah appears to be completely abandoned. In addition to caring for the orphans and the poor, there is also the category of widows which must be attended to as well. This is established in the Sunnah, for the following description was given of the Prophet ﷺ:

وَلَا يَأْنَفُ أَنْ يَمْشِيَ مَعَ الأَرْمَلَةِ وَالمِسْكِينِ فَيَقْضِي لَهُ الحَاجَةَ

"He never was prideful to be seen walking with the widow and orphan, and would accompany them until he fulfilled their need."

Likewise, in another noteworthy *ḥadīth*, the Prophet ﷺ is reported to have said:

السَّاعِي عَلَى الأَرْمَلَةِ وَالمِسْكِينِ كَالمُجَاهِدِ فِي سَبِيلِ اللهِ وَكَالقَائِمِ الذِي لَا يَفْتُرُ وَكَالصَّائِمِ الذِي لا يُفْطِرُ

"The [one who] strives in caring for the widows and the poor is like the one who strives in the path of Allah, and like the one who prays all night without sleeping and fasts all day without breaking it."

All of these rewards are assigned for the person who cares for the widow and the needy. Upon observing the corpus of religious texts on this issue, one will notice that the general theme is that a Muslim should always care and attend for the vulnerable people around him. This is why the Prophet ﷺ said: "Allah helps His servant as long as His servant helps his brother..." There is no doubt that for this category, the greatest reward can be found in aiding a widow, as her tragedy is unrivalled. This is especially the case if the widow is of old age, such that she cannot take care of herself properly. Related to this issue is the virtue found in taking care of and raising an orphan. Regarding this latter matter, the Prophet ﷺ said:

أَنَا وَكَافِلُ الْيَتِيمِ كَهَاتَيْنِ

"I and the one who cares for the orphan are like these two."

He then joined two of his fingers together to indicate the close proximity between them. This means that if a person helps a widow who tragically lost her husband by constantly caring and spending on her orphans, he will be close to the Prophet ﷺ in Paradise. In one of these narrations, the Prophet ﷺ specifically said that this caring for orphans can be for one's own children or for someone else's. So, the same reward mentioned in the *ḥadīth* will be attained regardless of whether the children are one's own or someone else's. This is because we know that charity (*ṣadaqah*) given to one's own family is greater than any other form of it. Obviously, a mother who takes care of her own children is not simply performing an act of charity. She is obtaining the reward of both charity and maintaining ties (*ṣilah*) with one's family members.

There are in fact a number of beautiful narrations (*āthār*) which mention the Prophet ﷺ seeing a woman racing with him on the Day of Judgement to the gates of Paradise. This particular woman cared for her children and raised them until they reached the age of maturity. Thus, this category encompasses some of the best people imaginable; no sensible person would give up the opportunity to serve people bestowed with the honour of being so close to the Prophet ﷺ. This is the first matter of immense importance which the Muslim nation must observe once again: serving the widows and being in their cause. Members of the community must ensure that they are taken care of and treat the maintenance of their well-being as a communal duty.

There was a brother—may Allah be pleased with him—who would anonymously send 500 dollars every single month to a local sister whose husband had passed away. That way, she could meet the needs of her family. To ensure his identity remained hidden, he would send the money through another person. That way, neither the sister nor myself could know the identity of this charitable brother. The generosity and sincerity of this brother towards this family was breathtaking; not only did he want to act upon the *ḥadīth* of the Prophet ﷺ, he also wanted to ensure his identity was never disclosed.

In sum, ensuring that the widow's needs are met so she can grieve properly is from the Sunnah of the Prophet ﷺ. To this effect there are several narrations which discuss how the widow is to grieve. Zaynab bint Abī Salamah ؓ narrated that three days after Abū Sufyān ؓ passed away, Umm Ḥabībah ؓ asked for some perfume, which she then applied on her forearms and cheeks. She then explained that she was not doing this out of any desire or impulse, but instead to abide by the Prophet's command, who said: "It is not permissible for a woman who believes in Allah and in the Last Day to abstain from adorning herself for more than three days, except in the case of the widow who mourns for four months and ten days." The latter form of waiting period is a special scenario, and is discussed by Allah ﷻ in *Sūrah al-Baqarah*.

Unfortunately, the waiting period is a matter which is surrounded with a lot of cultural innovations and practices which are not supported by the Prophetic Sunnah. What Allah teaches us in the Qur'ān is that the waiting period lasts for four months and ten days. However, as a special exception, the pregnant woman's waiting period expires the moment she gives birth to her child, even if this occurs a day after the death of her husband. But as long as she remains in her waiting period, she mourns the loss of her husband, and is required to spend the night in her home. Much of the Islamic law (*fiqh*) for the rulings regarding death and how to respond to it was legislated in the aftermath of the Battle of Uḥud, which had a huge impact on the Muslim community. For example, after this military encounter, the Prophet ﷺ saw some of the widows gathering outside during the day. He permitted them to continue their conversations during the day. However, during the night, he requested them to sleep inside the home where they first heard the news of their husband's death.

With regards to the waiting period, the woman is permitted to leave during the day to fulfil her needs. There is no problem with that whatsoever. In ideal circumstances, however, it would be optimal for members of the community to take care of her needs so she would not have to go out for herself. That way, she can take the time to properly grieve and be alone with herself. However, it is important to note that she must abstain from adorning herself and avoids any activities which may lead to marriage, such as meeting suitors and accepting proposals. None of these rules or regulations are harsh; neither do they enforce any form of punishment for the grieving widow. In fact, the only thing she is required to do is spend the night in the home of her husband. This should be observed as long as it is possible. In this particular matter I observe two different extremes. In some scenarios, I have noticed that this ruling is enforced even when the obligation can be waived. In other cases,

I have found people abstaining from it without a legitimate reason. The reality is that just like for all other issues of our religion, the correct course of action lies in the middle. For instance, if a person finds himself or herself in a state of dire need, then that will lift the ruling of prohibition. An example of this may be found in the case of an elderly woman who cannot stay alone at night, due to being unable to take care of her own needs. In such circumstances, she is permitted to live in the residence of her sister or another relative who could attend to her needs. Likewise, it may be the case that a woman's husband passes away during the performance of Hajj. This in fact happened in one of the Hajj groups which I was leading. If this occurs, a woman is not required to stay in the city of Makkah for four months and ten days. Instead, she is permitted to return to her home and spend the required waiting period there.

Of course, there are some individuals who do not observe the waiting period whatsoever. This of course is not something acceptable in normal circumstances. However, if a person faces circumstances which make the observance of this obligation during the night exceedingly difficult, then the ruling can be waived. Of course, during the day, there are no such restrictions and burdens. However, the community should take initiative and act like an extended family by serving her needs and alleviating her burdens so she can grieve in an appropriate way, which is free of any disturbances or obstructions. In fact, members of her community should see it as an opportunity and blessing to serve her.

The last point which should be discussed is that just like the issue of condolences, there are some cultural practices which unfortunately replace the Sunnah's prescription of ease with difficult commandments instead. Some of these invented rulings can actually pose a serious trial (*fitnah*) for a woman's steadfastness and commitment to her religion (*dīn*). For instance, there are some cultures which state that a woman should not smile at all throughout the entirety of the mourning period, which often lasts for four months and ten days. These cultural innovations introduce unnecessary hardships and difficulties for the mourning woman. The Sunnah, however, has a very simple and limited list of prohibitions. During the mourning period, a woman is only prohibited from adorning herself and sleeping outside her residence at night. She is permitted to go outside during the day to fulfil her needs. Afflicting this woman with additional burdens during the waiting period is a misguided emulation of practices implemented during the Period of Ignorance (*jāhiliyyah*). Instead of implementing that which is wrong, our priority as a community should be to address the responsibilities and needs of this woman during this period. That way, we can be instrumental in reviving a lost Sunnah.

The Prophet ﷺ said:
"The [one who] strives in caring for the widows and the poor is like the one who strives in the path of Allah, and like the one who prays all night without sleeping and fasts all day without breaking it."

14

Women Praying Janāzah

There are many sisters in our communities who have never had the chance to see the funeral procession of a fellow Muslim. They have never had the opportunity to see a deceased Muslim undergo the processes already discussed, such as having them be taken to their final resting place and be buried with the dirt being poured on them.

Death is always within reach, yet in a growing climate of materialism, people are always deluded by the false promises that this life provides. In the present world, we are encountering unforeseen levels of greed and materialism which are extremely harmful, and also causing us to assign unnecessary value to life. It is vital that we all make encounters with episodes of death, so we may be prepared to experience it personally ourselves when our appointed time arrives. This can be achieved by performing the ceremonial washing (*ghusl*) of the dead body, or being nearby someone when they are close to dying. Even being with a mourning family by comforting them through soothing words will prove spiritually beneficial; such actions help soften the heart.

But there is nothing which can match the emotional and spiritual experiences one undergoes while being inside a graveyard, or seeing someone be buried in front of them. Traditionally speaking, there is a difference of opinion (*ikhtilāf*) regarding the range of activities which women are permitted to participate in during the funeral, especially with regard to visiting the graveyard and witnessing the burial. This matter does deserve detailed treatment, as it encompasses several categories, with some matters being unanimously permitted, and others being unanimously prohibited. First and foremost, the performance of the funeral prayer (*ṣalāh al-janāzah*) is unanimously permitted for women, even in traditional Islamic law. This ruling applies in all circumstances, regardless of whether the prayer is done inside the *masjid* or outside. This ultimately then means that women who perform the funeral prayer will earn the same reward known as the *qīrāṭ*, which is equivalent to the size of Mount Uḥud. This is something which can be confirmed for women who partake in the prayer. On the other hand, wailing (*niyāḥah)* is absolutely prohibited for both genders, and actually harms the dead. In the time of the Prophet ﷺ, wailing was prohibited for both men and women. In the past Days of Ignorance (*jāhiliyyah*), after the death of a person people wailed loudly, slapped their cheeks, tore their clothes, and shouted words indicating their grief and displeasure. There were even professional wailers who were hired and asked to perform these activities after the death of a person. The Prophet ﷺ put an end to this practice by prohibiting it, and in fact cursed the people who wailed upon the death of someone. So far, two different practices have been evaluated, which have universal rulings for both genders. The first is the funeral prayer, which is permitted—and in fact encouraged—for both genders. On the other hand, wailing is absolutely prohibited for everyone.

There are then some actions which fall in between these two categories, such as following the funeral procession and visiting the graveyard. As for visiting graves, there is a narration which mentions that ʿĀ'ishah ﵂ was returning from the Baqīʿ graveyard. At this point, someone asked her, "Where are you coming from, O Mother of the Believers (*umm al-mu'minīn*)?" She mentioned that she had just visited the grave of her brother ʿAbd al-Raḥmān ﵁. The person then asked in surprise: "Was it not the case that the Prophet prohibited that?" ʿĀ'ishah ﵂ said:

نَعَمْ، كَانَ نَهَى، ثُمَّ أَمَرَ بِزِيَارَتِهَا

"Yes, the Prophet used to prohibit us, then he commanded us to visit them."

In this legally noteworthy *ḥadīth*, ʿĀ'ishah ﵂ was indicating that the original ruling of prohibition of visiting the graves applied to both men and women. During the time of this original prohibition there was a particular emphasis on women, since they were known to often wail while being at the grave as well. But after the Prophet ﷺ commanded his Companions to visit the graves, this did not shift the ruling to mere permissibility, but recommendation as well. This new ruling also applied to women as long as they properly observed the *ḥijāb*, did not frequently visit the graves, and abstained from wailing and mourning excessively. This view of permissibility is in fact adopted by a large group of scholars, who base their position on ʿĀ'ishah's narration.

Some of the scholars drew a distinction between following the funeral procession, as opposed to going to the graveyard alone. This differentiation is primarily based on a number of narrations, some of which are of contested authenticity. However, there is an authentic narration from Umm ʿAṭiyyah ﷺ, in which she said they were forbidden to follow the funeral processions (*janā'iz*), but this was not strictly enforced upon them. However, there is some ambiguity on when this ruling was implemented, for it may have been applied when visiting graves was prohibited as a whole or after the initial prohibition was abrogated. For this reason, the scholars concluded that following the funeral procession is disliked for women, which also seems to be the apparent import of Umm ʿAṭiyyah's report as well. The scholars differed on their lines of reasoning for why this ruling is justified. Some of them said that it is the practices of wailing and mourning which are frowned upon. Obviously, following the funeral procession is very likely to induce such reactions, as the woman is exposed to a tasking and distressing environment, as opposed to merely visiting the graveyard afterwards. Other scholars held the view that the ruling revolves around these different reactionary elements themselves; if a woman abstains from them, then she is permitted to accompany the funeral procession and witness the burial.

One of the main pieces of evidence cited by the scholars on this issue is a famous incident where the Prophet ﷺ came upon a woman that was weeping over her lost child. After approaching her, the Prophet ﷺ told her to observe patience. The woman responded harshly by saying: "What do you know about my tragedy (*muṣībah*)?" The Prophet ﷺ did not say anything in response, and merely walked away. Some of the people then asked the woman if she knew who she just addressed. She asked them to reveal his identity. They then told her that it was the Messenger of Allah ﷺ. She then immediately went to the Prophet ﷺ and apologised to him for her error. In response to her statement, the Prophet ﷺ said:

إِنَّمَا الصَّبْرُ عِنْدَ الصَّدْمَةِ الأُولَى

"True patience is at the first stroke of calamity."

Some of the scholars mentioned that the Prophet ﷺ made no remark concerning her presence or grief. Instead, through this remark the Prophet ﷺ was indicating the importance of observing patience for anyone who goes through such difficult moments. Merely upholding the basic legal requirements is not enough. Instead, during such moments Muslims must ensure they derive the full spiritual and religious benefits available.

It is vital that we all make encounters with episodes of death, so we may be prepared to experience it personally ourselves when our appointed time arrives. Even being with a mourning family by comforting them through soothing words will prove spiritually beneficial; such actions help soften the heart.

15

How Do I Move On?

You are not supposed to move on *from* them. Instead, strive to move forward *with* them. There is in fact no such thing as moving on. The Prophet ﷺ is the example and standard we are expected to emulate, and we know that he never moved on after Khadījah ﵂ passed away. Instead, he always cherished the priceless moments he shared with her. He kept her memory intact such that 'Ā'ishah ﵂ said: "I did not feel jealous of any of the wives of the Prophet as much as I did of Khadījah, even though I never met her." Yet the Prophet's constant mention and praise of Khadījah ﵂ was that which kept her name alive. Whenever the Prophet ﷺ sacrificed an animal or received the meat of a sacrifice from someone else, he would always send a share of it to Khadījah's friends. In addition, he would provide them gifts and other valuables. Whenever he heard the voice of her sister, he would rush to the door because she sounded just like her. He always thought about her. There is a statement from

ʿĀ'ishah which powerfully embodies the love that the Prophet continued to have for Khadījah:

كَأَنْ لَمْ يَكُنْ فِي الدُّنْيَا إِلَّا خَدِيجَةُ

"It was as if there was no woman in the world except Khadījah."

This statement is ironic and paradoxical, since Khadījah was already deceased at this point of time, yet her memory continued to occupy such a special place in his heart. This was to the extent that ʿĀ'ishah felt that no other person in the world mattered except her. In fact, the Prophet ﷺ would constantly remember her during his trials and victories. When he returned to Makkah, he pitched his tent at Ḥujjūn, which is in close proximity to Khadījah's grave. Without any doubt, the Prophet was always thinking about his deceased wife and making mention of her. The Prophet ﷺ was not crippled by his memory of Khadījah. Instead, her name was a motivator which spurred him to do good.

Furthermore, the Prophet ﷺ did not mistreat others as a result of the love he had towards Khadījah. For instance, he did not emotionally maltreat others due to the persisting love he had for his deceased wife. Instead, his experiences and memories of Khadījah were instrumental in expanding his heart; that way, he expanded his circle of loved ones.

In sum, the Prophet's experience with Khadījah is a vivid reminder that a person is not supposed to move on from his or her loved ones. Instead, they should move forward with them. This is a point which we must make sure to understand and implement properly. This is a theme which Allah reminds us of as well, since He orders us to remember death. Nothing allows us to remember death more frequently than the loss of a loved one with whom we had a close attachment. By remembering your dead loved one, you are also remembering death at the same time.

Thus, whenever you say *innā lillāhi wa innā ilayhi rāji'ūn* you are not just mourning their loss, but also reflecting on how close your own departure from this world is. Likewise, through your righteous actions on their behalf and these words of remembrance, you are actually keeping this person alive in this world. In essence, you can help leave for them a decorated and religiously significant legacy. When you observe the Companions, you will find that Zaynab bint Abī Salamah ﵂ was an extension of her parents Abū Salamah ﵁ and Umm Salamah ﵂. Furthermore, one notices how 'Abdullāh ibn Zubayr ﵁ became a brave and powerful warrior just like his father. Likewise, Usāmah ibn Zayd ﵁ followed his father's footsteps and became a warrior as well. In a similar fashion, 'Ā'ishah ﵂ was bestowed the title of *al-Ṣiddīqah bint al-Ṣiddīq*, which translates to "the truthful one, the daughter of the truthful one". She ended up acquiring the same title as her father, Abū Bakr ﵁. Fāṭimah ﵂ was the one who resembled the Prophet ﷺ the most in both religious conduct and the values she espoused. 'Abdullāh ibn 'Umar ﵁ and Ḥafṣah ﵂ extended the legacy of their father in an admirable way. After a relative or loved one passes away, you are ultimately the force that can keep them alive. Anything that causes you to remember death more and perform good deeds will ultimately bring you closer to Allah ﷻ.

As a living successor to that person, you should ask yourself, "What would my deceased loved one say to me if he or she had the opportunity to do so? Would he or she be pleased with my idleness and lethargy, where I am unable to fulfil anything? Or would he or she wish that I be an active and productive force for good?" Undoubtedly, he or she would prefer that you be from the latter category, since by being productive and doing good deeds, you are keeping his or her legacy alive. Likewise, by doing good and following the deceased's path of righteousness you will ensure that someone else will keep your memory alive after you die.

O Allah, forgive our living ones, deceased ones, present ones, absent ones, our little youngsters, elderly folk, our males, and our females. O Allah, whoever You have decreed to live amongst us, then let them live upon Islam. And whoever You decree to die, then have them die with full faith.

Āmīn